ELECTRIC AND HYBRID VEHICLES

2nd EDITION

A K Babu
Associate Professor
Department of Automobile Engineering
SRM Easwari Engineering College
Chennai-600089, Tamilnadu.

KHANNA BOOK PUBLISHING CO. (P) LTD.
Publisher of Engineering and Computer Books
4C/4344, Ansari Road, Darya Ganj, New Delhi-110002
Phone : 011-23244447-48 **Mobile:** +91-9910909320
E-mail : contact@khannabooks.com
Website : www.khannabooks.com

Dear Readers,

To prevent the piracy, this book is secured with HIGH SECURITY HOLOGRAM on the front title cover. In case you don't find the hologram on the front cover title, please write us to at contact@khannabooks.com or whatsapp us at +91-99109 09320 and avail special gift voucher for yourself.

Specimen of Hologram on front Cover title: 

Moreover, there is a SPECIAL DISCOUNT COUPON for you with EVERY HOLOGRAM.

How to avail this SPECIAL DISCOUNT:

Step 1: Scratch the hologram
Step 2: Under the scratch area, your "coupon code" is available
Step 3: Logon to www.khannabooks.com
Step 4: Use your "coupon code" in the shopping cart and get your copy at a special discount
Step 5: Enjoy your reading!

ISBN: 978-81-951231-5-5

Electric and Hybrid Vehicles
by Dr. A.K. Babu

First Edition: 2018
Second Edition: 2022
Reprint: 2024, 2025, **2026**

Published by:
Khanna Book Publishing Co. (P) Ltd.
CIN: U22110DL1998PTC095547

Visit us at: **www.khannabooks.com**
Write us at: **contact@khannabooks.com**

To view complete list of books, Please scan the QR Code: KPH

Printed in Bharat.

प्रो. एम.पी. पूनीयाँ
उपाध्यक्ष
Prof. M.P. Poonia
Vice-Chairman

सत्यमेव जयते

अखिल भारतीय तकनीकी शिक्षा परिषद्
(भारत सरकार का एक सांविधिक निकाय)
(शिक्षा मंत्रालय, भारत सरकार)
नेल्सन मंडेला मार्ग, वसंत कुंज, नई दिल्ली-110070
दूरभाष : 011-26131495
ई-मेल : vcm@aicte-india.org

ALL INDIA COUNCIL FOR TECHNICAL EDUCATION
(A STATUTORY BODY OF THE GOVT. OF INDIA)
(Ministry of Education, Govt. of India)
Nelson Mandela Marg, Vasant Kunj, New Delhi-110070
Phone : 011-26131495
E-mail : vcm@aicte-india.org

Foreword

Much like cell phones are now capable of doing more than making calls, cars can do much more than drive and park. In recent years, the automotive industry has worked hand-in-hand with major technology companies in order to deliver the most advanced, safest and most comfortable vehicles out there. Cars are becoming large smart devices with advanced emergency braking capabilities, mapping technology for autonomous driving, better fuel efficiency and cars as a service as a form of transportation.

With a view to enhance the employability skills and impart deep knowledge in Automobile Sector, AICTE with the assistance of industry-academia experts, has designed a curriculum in this area.

I am happy to know that Dr. A.K. Babu, a well-known author of automobile engineering books, has collaborated with a highly reputed publisher, M/s. Khanna Book Publishing Company Private Limited, to write as series of books on the subject of **"Automobiles"**.

Having written these books in a simple way in accordance with the requirements of AICTE, Dr. Babu has helped our students better understand these topics, as well as capture the plethora of employment opportunities available in this field.

The books are written according to the AICTE guidelines for the subject.

As a dedicated teacher in the field of Automobile Engineering, Dr. Babu's commitment and efforts in writing these series of books are highly appreciated. congratulate him for his contributions towards our higher education.

I wish the author, publisher as well as readers all the best!

(Prof. M.P. Poonia)

PREFACE

Stringent emissions standards and fuel consumption regulations have focused attention on the development of safe, clean, and highly efficient modes of transportation. It is well recognized that recent technological advances such as electric, hybrid electric and fuel cell-powered drive train technologies offer the most promising vehicle solutions to effectively address the pressing problems of conventional urban land transportation in the near future.

Readers will find that this second edition is a storehouse of useful and interesting information about electric and hybrid vehicles.

The book reviews the core electrical and electronic principles before moving on to an in-depth discussion of electric vehicles and hybrid electric vehicles. The contents of the book are laid out in twenty five well-structured chapters. The book deals with the fundamentals, electric vehicles (EVs), hybrid electric vehicles (HEVs), and fuel cell vehicles (FCVs) in a concise and lucid manner. It comprehensively covers vehicle performance, configuration, and control strategy for different conventional and modern vehicles.

The layout of the book has been designed in a student-friendly manner to facilitate easy learning and I hope that the information presented here will enrich the knowledge base of young readers. Comments, suggestions and feedback are always welcome.

Author

CONTENTS

1 Fundamentals of Electricity

UNIT OUTCOMES

Upon successful completion of this module, the student will be able to:

1. Study the elements of electricity.
2. Identify the different electrical circuits
3. Demonstrate the usage of DC measuring instruments
4. Practice the different action of electric current.
5. Get exposed to voltage generation methods.

FUNDAMENTALS OF ELECTRICITY

The components of the electric vehicles are applications of the various actions made possible by the flow of electricity. Before taking up the construction and operation of these various electric vehicle components, the fundamentals of electricity and electronics will first be reviewed.

ELECTRICITY

Electricity is a form of energy and is produced by the movement of small atomic particles known as electrons. It can be easily transmitted or converted to other forms, such as mechanical or heat energy. To transmit electricity, conductors such as copper, steel, carbon or an electrolyte are used. Insulators such as rubber, porcelain or bakelite are used to prevent electrical leakage from conductors.

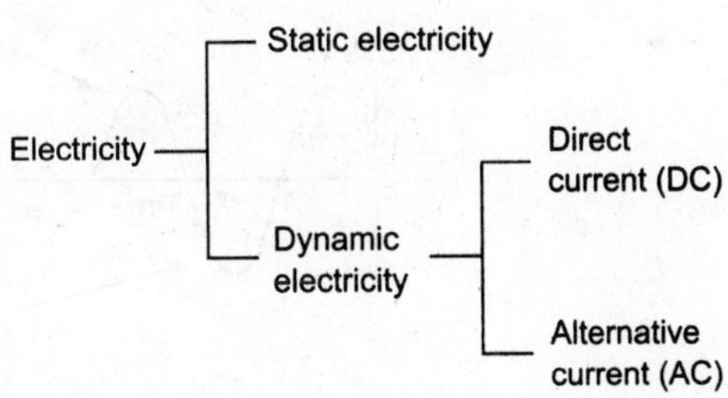

There are two kinds of electricity: static and dynamic. Dynamic electricity can be further divided into direct current (DC) and alternating current (AC).

Static Electricity

When a non-conductive substance such as a glass rod is rubbed with a silk cloth, the surfaces of both the rod and the cloth become charged with electricity, one positively and one negatively. Unless the two materials touch, or are connected by a conductor, the electrical charge will remain in the glass rod and silk cloth. Since it does not move, this type of electricity is called static electricity.

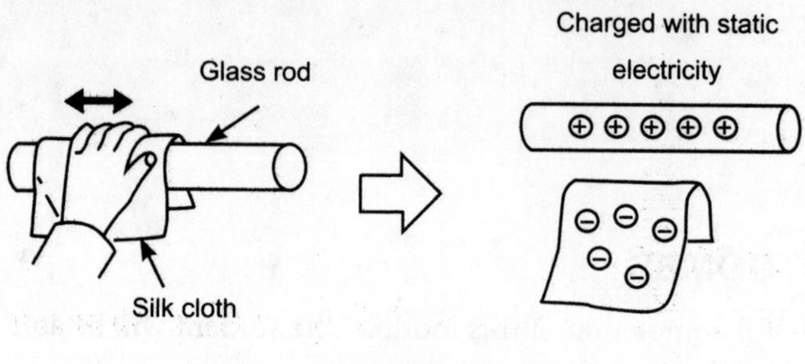

Fig. 1.1 Static electricity

In terms of free electron, static electricity refers to a state in which free electrons are separated from their atoms and do not move about on the surface of the substance.

Dynamic Electricity

Dynamic electricity refers to a state in which there is a flow of free electrons, i.e. electrons that are separated from their atoms and moving about inside the conductive substance.

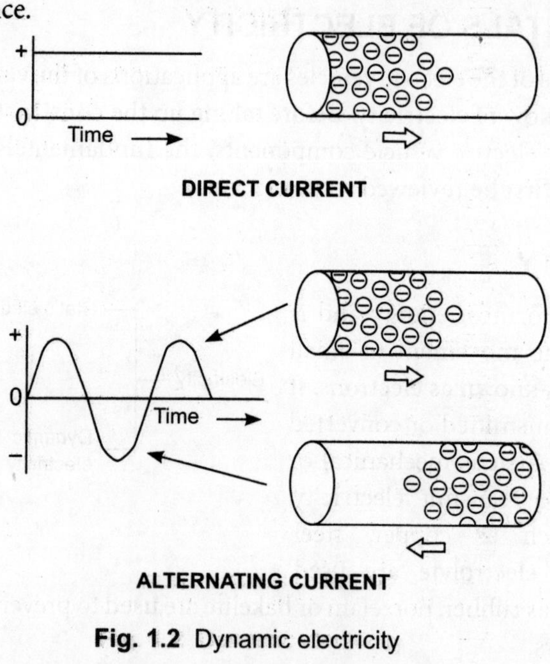

Fig. 1.2 Dynamic electricity

When the free electrons are moving in a constant direction, the state of dynamic electricity is called direction current (DC). When the direction of motion and the size of the current vary periodically with time, the state of dynamic electricity is called alternating current (AC).

ELEMENTS OF ELECTRICITY

The three elements of electricity are voltage, current and resistance.

Current

Electric current is a flow of electrons and is measured in amps, (short for amperes). The amp is a measure of flow rate. In other words how much electricity is flowing per second.

Fig. 1.3 Current

1 amp = 6,240,000,000,000,000,000 electrons per second

In electronic circuits a current of one amp is quite large, so often the milli-amp is used instead. A milli-amp (mA) is a thousandth of an amp (A).

Voltage

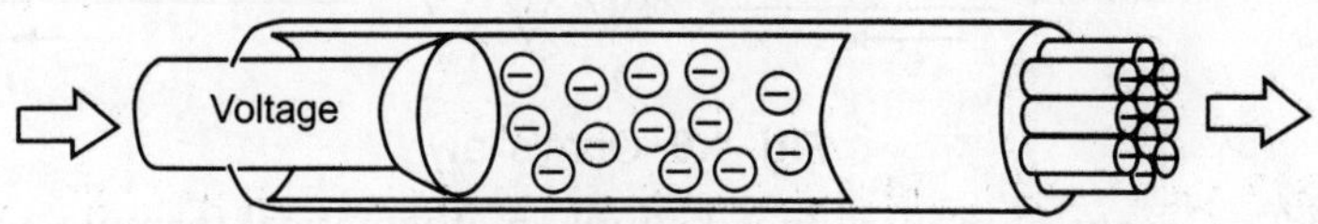

Fig. 1.4 Voltage

Electricity does not flow through a wire unless it is pushed. There has to be an electrical pressure and this pressure is called voltage and is measured in Volts. The symbol is V. It is also called electrical pressure, and electromotive force (emf). This pressure can be provided by a battery, or it can be produced by a generator.

Resistance

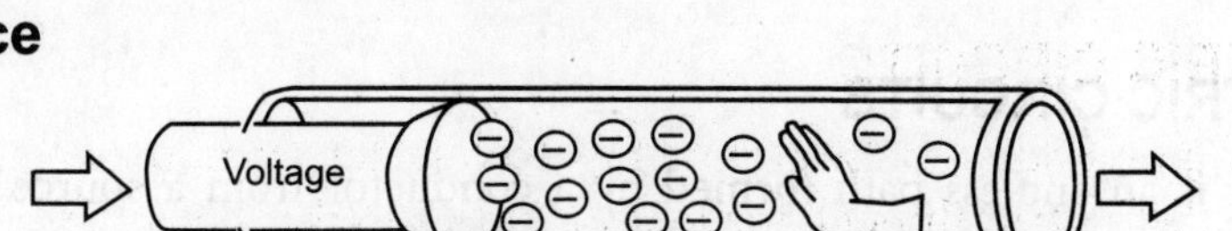

Fig. 1.5 Resistance

The rate that the electrons pass around the circuit (i.e. the amount of current) is dependent not only on the force (voltage) but also by how much resistance there is in the circuit. Resistance is measured in ohms (W).

In the case of electricity, a same conductor will allow better current flow when its diameter becomes larger due to less resistance. When it becomes longer, its resistance increases so that the current gets weaker. That is, the resistance of a conductor is directly proportional to its length and inversely proportional to its cross-sectional area. Because in a car the same 12V battery powers all circuits, the only way that current can vary is by varying the resistance.

The conductor resistance normally changes with the temperature. The resistance also varies with the conductor material. The resistances of metal conductors increase when the temperature rises, but resistances of carbon and aqueous solutions decrease. A good conductor will have small resistance, whereas the resistance of insulating material will be enormous.

OHM'S LAW

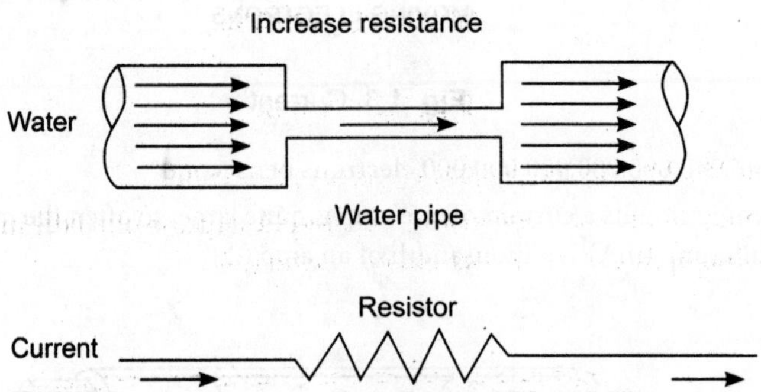

Fig. 1.6 Ohm's law

In 1827, George ohm introduced simple mathematical formula, which relates voltage, current, and resistance. This formula is called Ohm's law. Ohm's law says voltage is equal to current times resistance. A force of 1V is required to push a current of 1A through a resistance of 1Ω.

$V = I \times R$ Where, V = Voltage in volts

I = Current in amperes

R = Resistance in ohms

ELECTRIC CIRCUITS

A circuit is an endless path formed by a conductor from a source of electrical supply to the control, through the load, and back to the source. There are various types of electrical circuits used in the modern automobile, among them the series, and parallel circuits.

Series circuit

In a series circuit, there is only one current path. The same battery current flows through each component. A breakage in the path would cease the function of all the equipments.

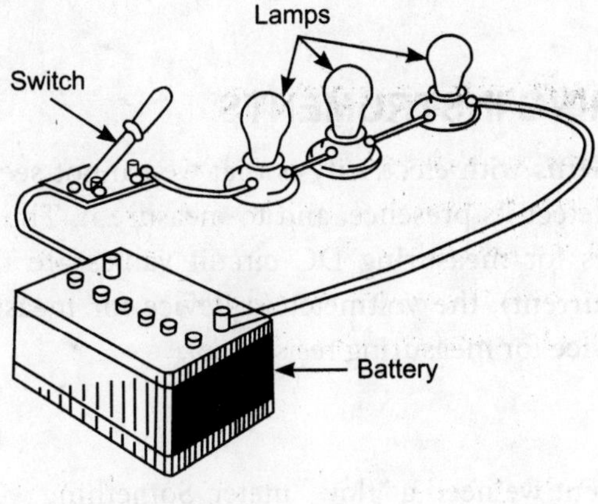

Fig. 1.7 Series circuit

The total resistance in a series circuit is the sum of the individual resistors. This is written as:

$$R_{total} =$$

$R_1 + R_2 + R_3$

Parallel circuit

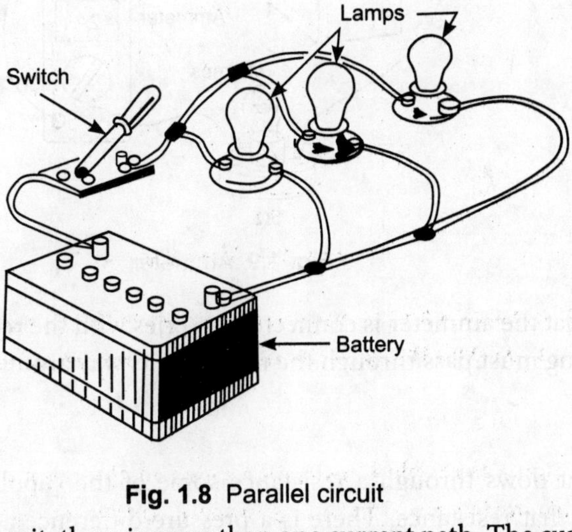

Fig. 1.8 Parallel circuit

In a parallel circuit, there is more than one current path. The current splits up, with the greater current flowing through the smallest resistance. A breakage in any one path would not interfere with the operation of the remainder of the units in the circuit.

The total resistance in a parallel circuit is found by using the formula:

$$R_{\text{total}} = \frac{1}{\frac{1}{R_1} + \frac{1}{R_2} + \frac{1}{R_3}}$$

DC MEASURING INSTRUMENTS

One of the problems with electricity is that we cannot see it. We have to rely on instruments to detect its presence, and to measure it. The three most commonly used instruments for measuring DC circuit values are the ammeter (a device for measuring current), the voltmeter (a device for measuring voltage) and the ohmmeter (a device for measuring resistance).

Ammeter

To measure current we need a "flow" meter. Something we can insert so that the current will pass through and it will display the rate of flow. To work, it has to have a very low resistance so that the current can pass through without the meter itself restricting the current flow. This type of meter is called an ammeter. To use it the circuit must be broken and the meter inserted.

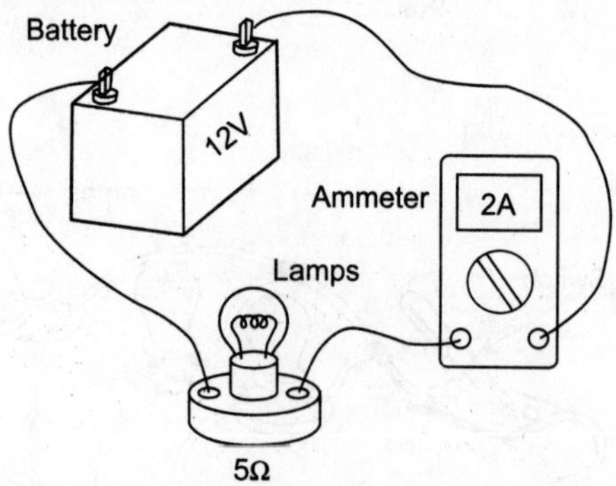

Fig. 1.9 Ammeter

Notice that the ammeter is connected in series with the rest of the circuit. Any current flowing must pass through the meter on its way around the circuit.

Voltmeter

When current flows through a resistance some of the supply pressure (voltage) is lost across that resistance. There is a pressure difference across the resistance. Therefore a voltage difference is found across components. To measure it the voltmeter has to be connected across the component (i.e. in parallel with it).

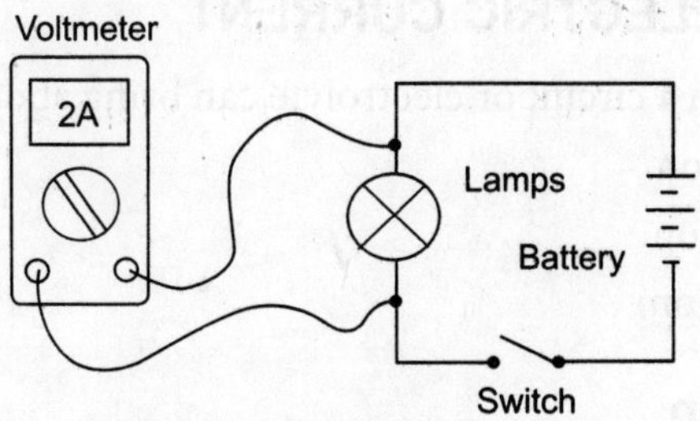

Fig. 1.10 Voltmeter

Ohmmeter

When measuring resistance the ohmmeter provides the voltage to pass a current through the components. From the current flowing, the meter works out the resistance. It is therefore important that there are no other currents flowing. The component to be measured must therefore be disconnected from its circuit first.

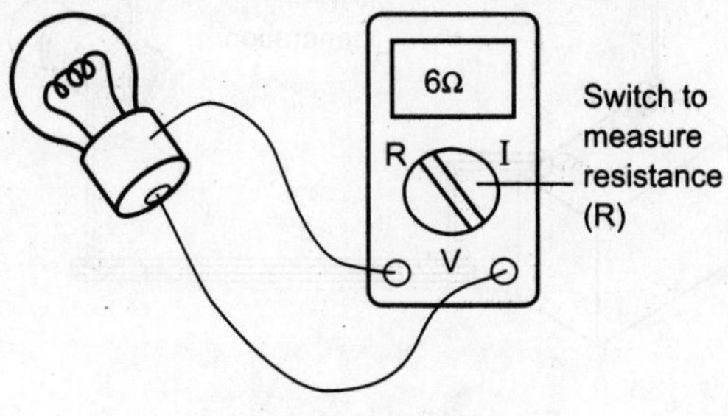

Fig. 1.11 Ohmmeter

Multimeter

Most meters used for measuring DC circuit values by technicians are multipurpose meters or multimeters. They are generally designed to measure voltage, resistance, and current. Therefore, a multimeter is often called a volt-ohm-milliammeter (VOM), because it can measure volts, ohms, and milliamperes.

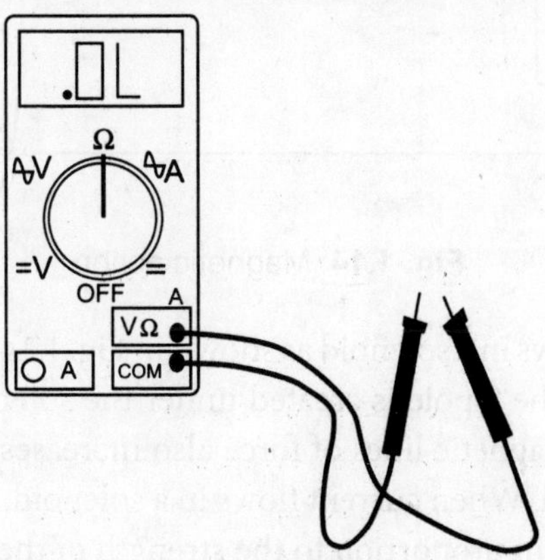

Fig. 1.12 Multimeter

ACTIONS OF ELECTRIC CURRENT

A current flowing in a circuit or electrolyte can bring about the following circuits:

1. Heat generation
2. Magnetic action
3. Chemical action

Heat generation

When current is applied to the cigarette lighter in an automobile, the nichrome wire in the cigarette lighter heats up and becomes red. This is because the electric energy is consumed by the nichrome wire's resistance and converted into heat energy. The action which generates heat when current flows in a resistance is called the heat generating action of current.

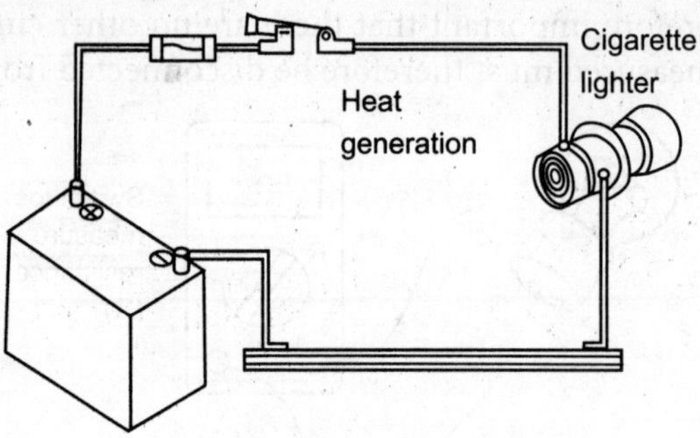

Fig. 1.13 Heat generation

Magnetic action

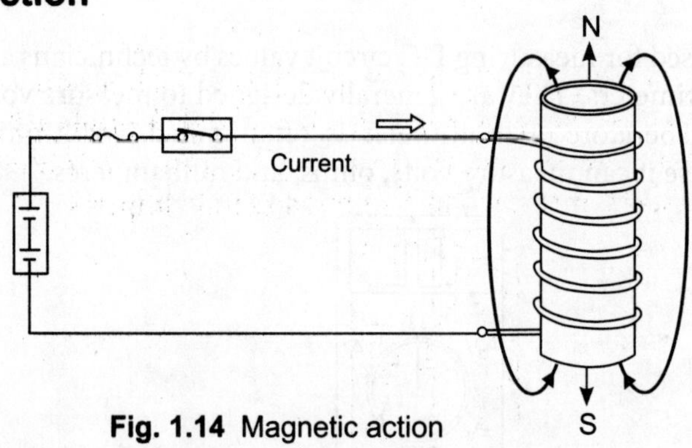

Fig. 1.14 Magnetic action

When current flows in a solenoid as shown in Fig. 1.14, the direction of the magnetic flux is such that the S pole is created under the solenoid, and the N pole above it. The number of magnetic lines of force also increases in proportion to the number of turns of the coil. When current flows in a solenoid, the number of magnetic lines of force increases in proportion to the strength of the current.

Chemical action

When two metal plates are placed in an aqueous solution of salt or sulphuric acid, etc., and a lamp and battery are connected by wires to the plates, as shown in Fig. 1.15, the lamp will light up. This proves that an electrical circuit has been formed, and current is flowing through the liquid solution.

When electricity flows in such a solution, chemical action takes place on the surfaces of the metal plates. Batteries are charged by a chemical reaction such as this.

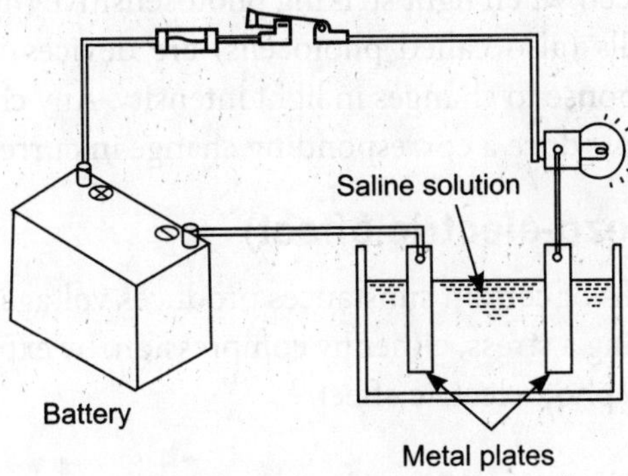

Fig. 1.15 Chemical action

VOLTAGE GENERATION

The voltage can be generated by:

Electromagnetic induction

In 1831, Michael Faraday demonstrated that magnetism could produce electricity. When a conductor moves through a magnetic field at right angles to the lines of magnetic force, the conductor is said to be cutting the magnetic lines of force and a voltage is induced in the conductor. The amount of voltage generated can be increased by increasing the strength of the magnetic field and by increasing the speed of the motion. Induced voltages are created by generators and alternators.

Electro-chemical cells

Electrochemical cells are the most compact sources of electric power. They produce electricity as a result of chemical actions inside the cell. When the cell is made, it is packed with chemical compounds that are ready to react together. As the current is drawn from the cell the chemical reaction occurs. Current can be obtained from the cell until the chemicals have completed their reaction and no more of the original compounds are left.

Heat (thermo element)

Voltage is produced by heating the joint (junction) where two unlike metals are joined. It may be noted that while doing so, one of the two metals is always maintained at lower temperature. This kind of voltage (emf) generation is common in thermo couple.

Light (photoelectric cells)

Voltage is produced when light striking photosensitive (light sensitive) substances. Photoelectric cells (also called photocells) are devices which produce electrical variations in response to changes in light intensity. Any change in light diversity or wavelength will produce a corresponding change in current, voltage, or resistance.

Pressure (piezo-electric effect)

Squeezing crystals of certain substances produces voltage. The effect of producing a voltage by placing a stress, either by compression, by expansion or by twisting, on a crystal is called photoelectric effect.

CONTROL DEVICES

Control devices are used to "turn on" or "turn off" or "vary" current flow in an electrical circuit. Control devices include a variety of switches, relays, solenoids, and variable resistors. Electronic control devices include capacitors, diodes, and transistors.

Switch

A switch is the most common circuit control device. Switches usually have two or more sets of contacts. Opening these contacts is called "break" or "open" the circuit, Closing the contacts is called "make" or "completing" the circuit.

Relay

A relay is simply a remote-control switch, which uses a small amount of current to control a large amount of current.

Solenoid

A solenoid is an electromagnetic switch that converts current flow into mechanical movement.

Variable resistor

Variable resistor is a resistor of which the ohmic resistance value can be adjusted either mechanically (potentiometer, rheostat) or electronically (digital potentiometer).

The potentiometer and rheostat are the two configurations that can be used in electronic circuits and components to achieve a variable voltage and current values.

REVIEW QUESTIONS

1. What is an electric current?
2. What is an electromotive force?
3. What is electrical resistance?
4. Name and describe two types of electricity.
5. Define a free electron.
6. What is a conductor?
7. What is an insulator?
8. What is the formula for electrical power?
9. How a resistance can be measured?
10. Define Ohm's law.
11. Define the following terms: (a) electric circuit, (b) volt, (c) ampere, (d) short circuit, (e) open circuit.
12. Explain the differences between a series and a parallel circuit.
13. Why is it important that all the lights on a vehicle be wired in parallel?
14. What effects may be produced by an electric current?

2 Fundamentals of Electronics

UNIT OUTCOMES

Upon successful completion of this module, the student will be able to:

1. Study different types of electronic devices.
2. Identify the different types of semiconductor devices
3. Study different types of transistors
4. Get exposed to microcomputer
5. Identify the input and output devices.

Now-a-days, not only industrial machinery (robots, etc), but also many home appliances and even toys operate by means of electronic devices called integrated circuits (ICs) and microcomputers. These ICs and microcomputers are built of such basic electronic components as transistors and diodes.

Electronic devices have now partially or completely replaced the mechanical devices that have been used up until present. This has made it possible to construct devices to do the same jobs as mechanical devices, but which are much more compact, efficient, and reliable than their mechanical equivalents, and to design devices having many increased capabilities to do totally new jobs.

Modern automobiles too now use many different types of electronic devices, which allow the automobile's fuel economy, reliability, comfort, and safety to be greatly improved in comparison with conventional mechanical control systems.

SEMICONDUCTORS

A semiconductor is a material having an electrical resistance higher than that of conductors such as copper or iron, but lower than that of insulators such as glass or rubber. A semiconductor has the following properties:

(a) As its temperature rises, its electrical resistance changes.
(b) When mixed with certain other substances, its electrical conductivity rises.
(c) Its resistance changes greatly when it is struck by light, and it emits (gives off) light when an electrical current is passed through it.

The two most commonly used semiconducting materials are germanium (Ge) and silicon (Si). However, in their pure state, there are not suitable for practical use as semiconductors. For this reason, they must be doped, that is, they must have slight amounts of impurities added to them to enhance their effectiveness.

DIODES

Semiconductor diodes are made of an n-type semiconductor joined to a p-type semiconductor. There are several types of diode.

Fig. 2.1 Diode

(a) Ordinary rectifying diode
(b) Zener diode
(c) Light-emitting diode (LED)
(d) Photodiode

Rectifying Diode

A rectifying diode allows a low-voltage current to flow through it if current flow is from the p-side to the n-side (forward biased), but stops current from flowing if it is from the n-side to the p-side (reverse biased).

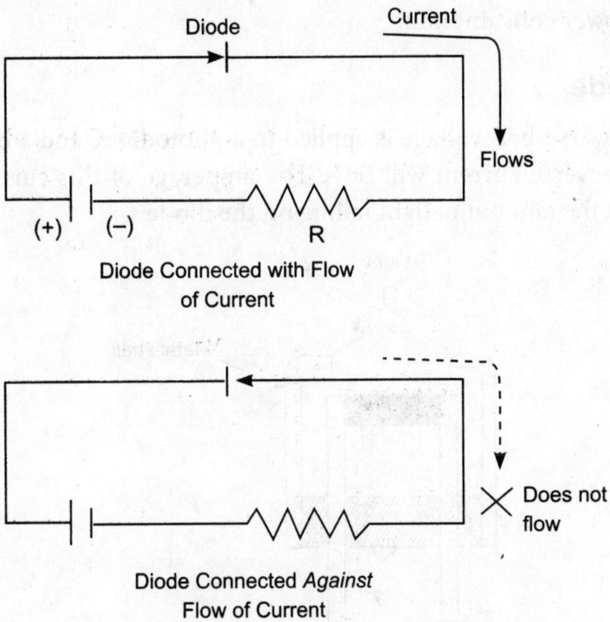

Fig. 2.2 Rectifying diode

Zener Diode

The Zener diode is like an ordinary diode in that it allows current to flow in the forward direction. However, it differs from an ordinary diode in that its reverse-bias breakdown voltage is much lower than that of an ordinary rectifying diode. This allows it to be used in low-voltage circuits, such as those found in automobiles.

The Zener diode is symbolized as follows:

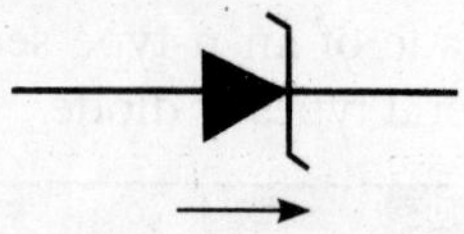

Fig. 2.3 Zener diode

Light-Emitting Diode (LED)

The light-emitting diode is an n-p junction diode that emits light when a current is passed through it in the forward direction. The LED is symbolized as follows:

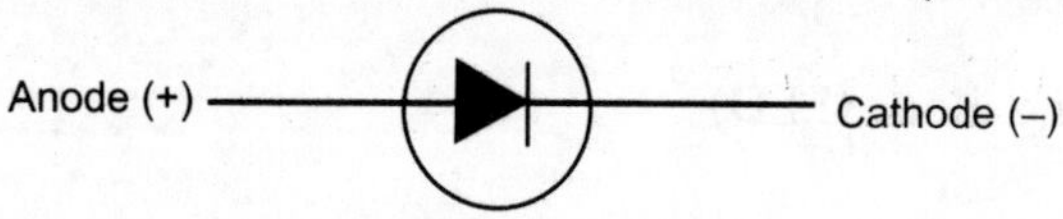

Fig. 2.4 LED

The LED has the following characteristics:

(a) Longer life and cooler operation than an ordinary light bulb.

(b) Operation possible at a lower voltage (about 3 V).

(c) Low power consumption.

Photo Diode

If a certain reverse-bias voltage is applied to a photodiode and a light is shone on the diode, a reverse current will flow. The amperage of this current will vary in proportion to the amount of light falling on the diode.

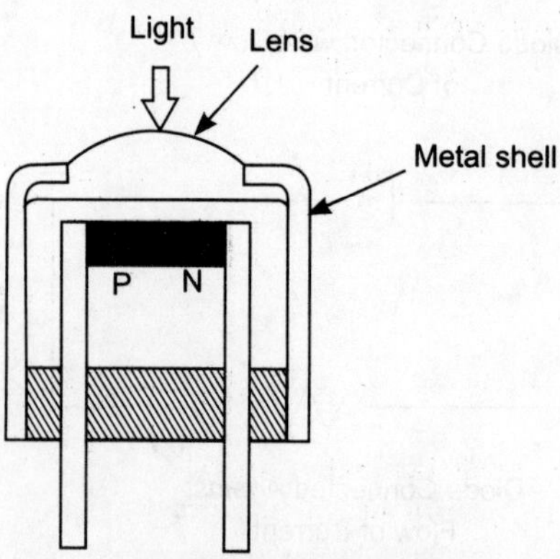

Fig. 2.5 Photo diode

TRANSISTORS

There are many different types of transistor, but here we will discuss only two of them: the ordinary transistor and the photo transistor.

Ordinary Transistor

Ordinary transistors come in two varieties: npn and pnp. The npn transistor is composed of a p-type semiconductor sandwiched between two n-type semiconductors, while the pnp type is composed of a n-type semiconductor between two p-type semiconductors.

In either case, an electrode is attached to each substrate (layer of semiconducting material).

Ordinary transistors have two basic functions or uses.; they can act either as signal amplifiers or as switches.

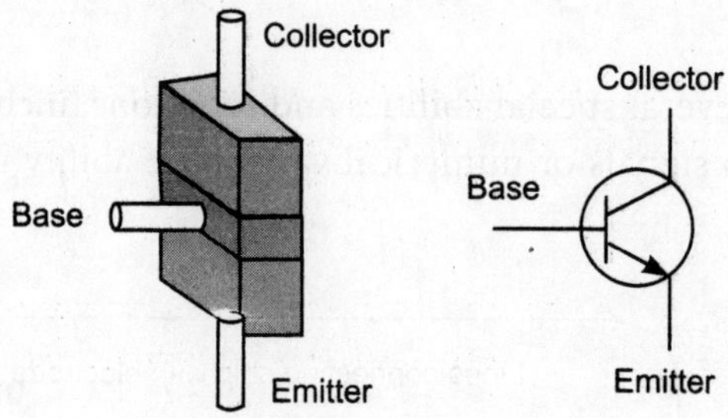

NPN TRANSISTOR

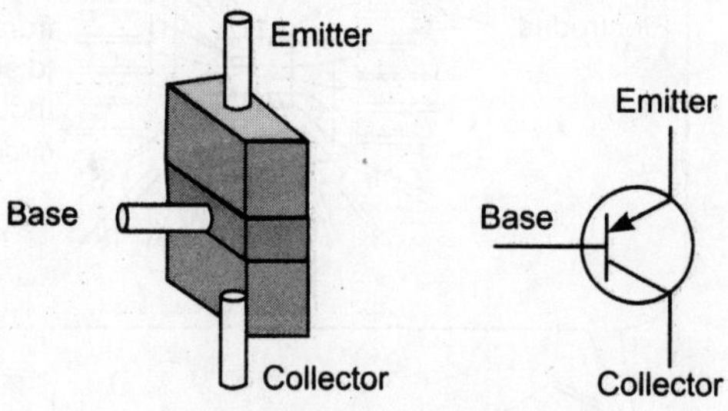

NPN TRANSISTOR

Fig. 2.6 Transistors

Photo Transistor

When light is allowed to shine on a photo transistor, it is converted into an electrical current. In an automobile, this type of transistor is used, for example, in conjunction with a LED as a vehicle speed sensor.

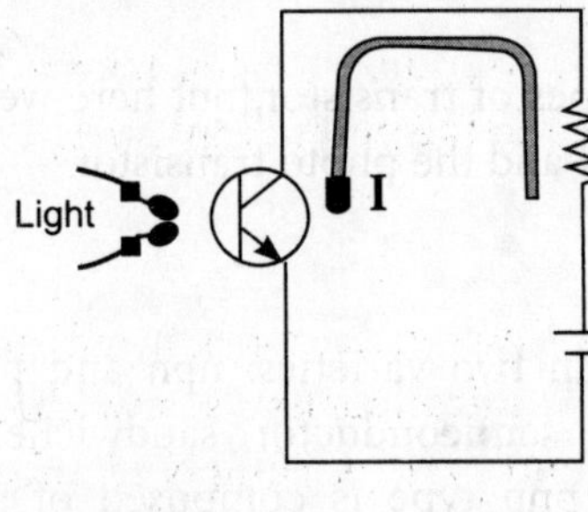

Fig. 2.7 Photo transistor

INTEGRATED CIRCUITS (IC'S)

An integrated circuit (IC) is a combination of from several to several thousand electrical circuits that are made up of transistors, diodes, capacitors, resistors, etc., built into or onto a several millimetre square silicon chip and packaged in a ceramic or plastic package.

A single IC has several special abilities and functions, including the ability to logically compare two signals or numerical values, the ability to amplify an input voltage, etc.

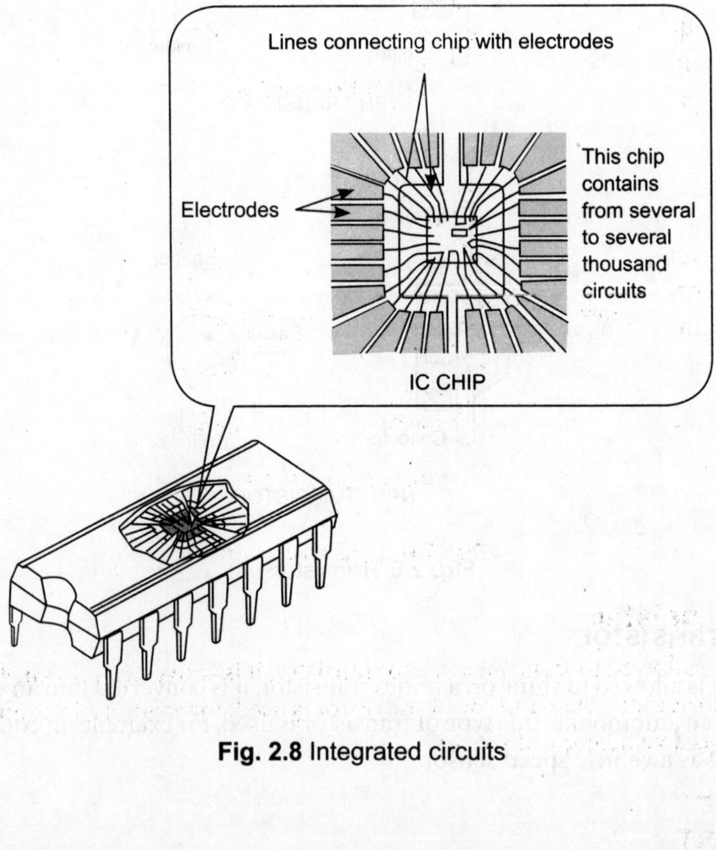

Fig. 2.8 Integrated circuits

MICROCOMPUTER

There are many different types and sizes of computers in use at present. The largest type is called a main-frame computer and is used in factories, large offices, etc. This type usually occupies one or more large rooms. The smallest type of computer is called a microcomputer or microprocessor and is used in household appliances, games, automobiles, etc. This type can usually be contained on a few tiny chips.

All computers, regardless of their size or type, consist of at least the following devices:

1. Central processing unit (CPU)
    - Registers
    - Arithmetic and logic unit (ALU)
    - Control unit
2. Memory (Backup storage unit)
3. Input devices
4. Output devices

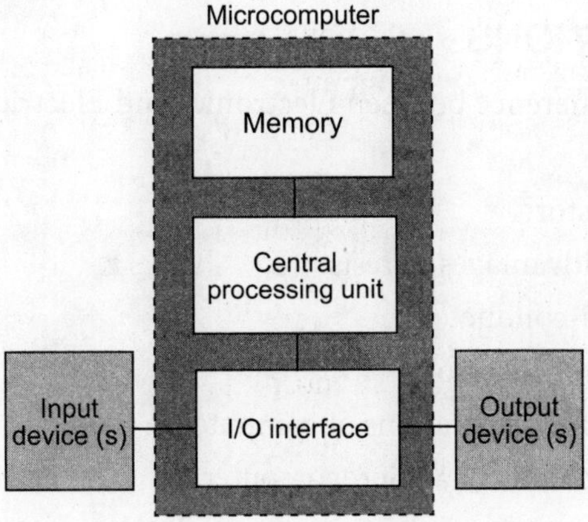

Fig. 2.9 Microcomputer

Central Processing Unit (CPU)

The CPU is so called because it is the functional center of the computer and is used to process data.

Memory

Memory (or storage) is a general term referring to the various storage devices in which are stored programs, input data, and data that are the results of the calculations and logical operations performed by the CPU.

I/O Interface

The I/O interface converts input data (data that is input into the computer from a input device) into a form that is recognizable by the CPU and storable by memory. It also reconverts output data into a form that is recongnizable by the output device.

Input devices

These are devices that input data into the computer. In an ordinary computer, these include keyboards, punched card readers, etc. In an automobile, these may include various sensors (speed sensor, coolant temperature sensor, etc) and switches (brake switch, overdrive switch).

Output devices

These are devices that perform various operations under the control of the CPU. In an ordinary computer, these may be a monitor screen, printer, etc. In an automobile, these may be a digital speedometer, fuel injectors, etc.

REVIEW QUESTIONS

1. What is the difference between Electronics and Electrical?
2. What is diode?
3. What is transistor?
4. What are the advantages of resistors?
5. What is a semi-conductor?
6. What is a microprocessor?
7. What are the basic operations of computer?
8. List out components of a microcomputer.

3 ELECTRIC VEHICLE EVOLUTION

UNIT OUTCOMES

Upon successful completion of this module, the student will be able to:

1. Get exposed to evolution of EVs.
2. Study the history of EVs

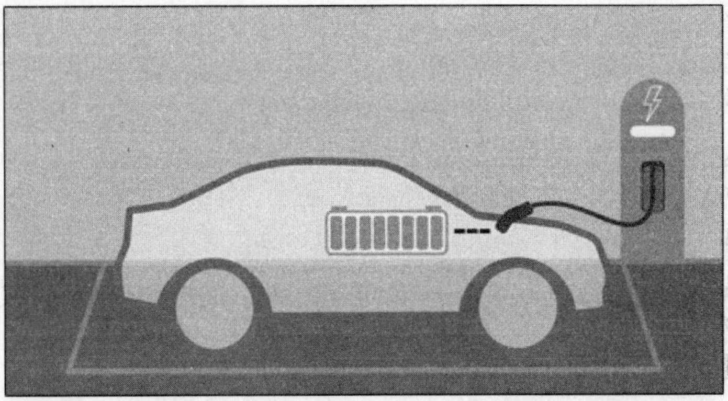

1828: Hungarian inventor Ányos Jedlik, who had invented an early electric motor, builds a small, model car powered by this motor.

1834: Vermont blacksmith Thomas Davenport and his wife Emily build a small, model electric car that runs on a circular, electrified track.

1835: In the Netherlands, Professor Sibrandus Stratingh of Groningen and his assistant, Christopher Becker, build a small electric car powered by primary cells (non-rechargeable batteries).

1837: Thomas & Emily Davenport, and colleague Orange Smalley, receive the first American patent for an electric machine/motor.

1837 & 1841: Large-scale "electric cars" are finally built by chemist Robert Davidson of Aberdeen. Powered by galvanic cells, the larger one, built in 1841, can pull 6 tons at 4 miles per hour for about 1½ miles. It weighs 7 tons.

1859: French physicist Gaston Planté invents the lead-acid battery, which actually makes practical electric cars a possibility. (Lead-acid batteries are still used in some electric cars today, and are used in gas-powered cars to help start the engines. However, most modern electric cars use lithium-ion batteries. The lead-acid batteries used to start cars are still very similar to what Gaston created.)

1870: Sir David Salomon developed a car with a light electric motor and heavy storage batteries. Driving speed and range were poor.

1881: French scientist Camille Alphonse Faure greatly improves the design of lead-acid batteries, increasing their capacity substantially. This leads to industrial-scale production of lead-acid batteries.

1881: An electric tricycle built by Gaston Planté is displayed at the International Exhibition of Electricity in Paris.

1881: Parisian engineer and carriage builder Charles Jeantaud, with the help of Camille Alphonse Faure, builds an electric car using a Tilbury-style buggy, a Gramme motor, and the Fulmen battery.

1881: Englishmen William Ayrton & John Perry build an electric tricycle, the first vehicle to use electric lights. It uses lead acid cells, has a range of 10 to 25 miles, and has a maximum speed of 9 mph.

1884: English inventor Thomas Parker builds in first practical production electric car in London. He uses "high-capacity" rechargeable batteries that he designed.

1884: Andrew Riker, develops an electric trike using lead-sulphuric acid batteries that has 25 miles of range.

1886: Historical records indicate that an electric-powered taxicab, using a battery with 28 cells and a small electric motor, was introduced in England.

1888: Immisch & Company built a four-passenger carriage, powered by a one-horsepower motor and 24-cell battery, for the Sultan of the Ottoman Empire. In the same year, Magnus Volk in Brighton, England made a three-wheeled electric car.

1888: Andrew Riker forms the Riker Electric Vehicle Company, which is based in Elizabeth Port, New Jersey.

1888: Philip Pratt demonstrates an electric tricycle built for him by Fred M. Kimball of Fred M. Kimball Company. Despite Riker's electric trike being built a few years earlier, many say that Pratt's electric trike is the first in the US, and Pratt is often given the title, "father of the American electric automobile."

1888: The first electric car in Germany is built by Andreas Flocken.

1888: Elwell-Parker Company and rivals merge in England to form the Electric Construction Corporation. The Electric Construction Corporation thus gains a monopoly on the production of electric cars in the coming decade.

1890-1891: The first American electric car is built by William Morrison of Des Moines, Iowa. The 6-passenger wagon can travel up to 23 km/h (14 mph). The car may also be the first land vehicle steered with a wheel. Morrison, a chemist, moved to Iowa from Scotland in 1880.

1890–1910: Period of significant improvements in battery technology, specifically with development of the modern lead-acid battery by H. Tudor and nickel-iron battery by Edison and Junger.

1893: William Morrison's electric car is shown at the "World's Colombian Exposition" in Chicago, seen by basically everyone who would become influential in the early years of electric vehicle development.

1894: Louis Antoine Krieger begins building electric "horseless carriages" in Paris. They use regenerative braking, with the captured energy stored in a battery and later used to help power the motor.

1894: Mechanical engineer Henry G. Morris and chemist Pedro G. Salom build the first "successful" electric car. With backgrounds in the dwindling battery streetcar market, Morris and Salom develop the "Electrobat" like a small battery streetcar. It has a top speed of 15 mph and uses a lead acid battery. It goes into production the following year, 1895.

1895: The first known US auto race is won by an electric vehicle.

1896: The first car dealer is set up in the US. It only sells electric vehicles.

1896: Morris and Salom build a 2-seat "Electric Road Wagon" and form the "Electric Carriage and Wagon Company," apparently the first electric car company in the US. Developed as coupes and hansoms for New York City taxis, the Electric Road Wagons each have rear-wheel steering, two 1/2 hp motors, 44 lead-acid cells, and a range of 30 miles.

1896: To overcome range limitations and lack of charging infrastructure, a battery exchange (battery swap) service is proposed. Implemented by Hartford Electric Light Company, the service is initially available for electric trucks.

1897: A fleet of electric vehicle taxis is brought to London by Walter C. Bersey. They receive the nickname "Hummingbirds" because of the light humming sound they make.

1897: A fleet of electric hansom cabs is brought to New York City by Samuel's Electric Carriage and Wagon Company.

1897: The first car with power steering is built. It's an electric car.

1897: The London Electric Cab Company began regular service using cars designed by Walter Bersey. The Bersey Cab, which used a 40-cell battery and 3 horsepower electric motor, could be driven 50 miles between charges.

1897: The Pope Manufacturing Company of Hartford, Connecticut, built around 500 electric cars over a two-year period.

1898: Dr. Ferdinand Porsche, 23 years old, builds his first car, the Lohner Electric Chaise. It has a hub motor at each driving wheel and is reportedly the first front-wheel-drive car in the world.

1898: Count Gaston de Chasseloup-Laubat of Paris sets the first known speed record in a car, going faster than any human before at 39.245 mph (62.8 km/h) in his electric Jeantaud. This earns him the nickname "Electric Count." Incidentally, the world record lasts for just a few days before being beaten by another electric vehicle.

1899: Camille Jenatzy and Count Gaston de Chasseloup-Laubat trade speed records several times throughout the year, ending in Camille Jenatzy breaking the 100 km/h (62 mph) speed barrier in an electric vehicle. He reaches a top speed of 105.88 km/h (65.79 mph). Jenatzy's vehicle is named La Jamais Contente ("The Never Satisfied"),

1899: Riker Electric Vehicle Company, Electric Carriage and Wagon Company, Electric Storage Battery, and Samuel's Electric Carriage and Wagon Company merge to form the "Electric Vehicle Company," attempting to create a monopoly in the US electric vehicle market.

1899: MIT electrical & mechanical engineering graduate Clinton Edgar Woods incorporates Woods Motor Vehicle Company, 3 years after forming American Electric Vehicle Company, which then became Waverly Company.

1899: The Baker Electric, the first production electric car, is born. It is produced by Baker Motor Vehicle Company.

1900: 38% of US automobiles, 33,842 cars, are powered by electricity (40% by steam, and 22% by gasoline).

1901: Thomas Edison patents the nickel-iron battery.

1902: Dr. Ferdinand Porsche builds second car, a hybrid with an electric range of 40 miles.

1902: Walter Baker goes 104 mph (167 km/h) in his electric "Road Torpedo," setting a new world speed record in Ormond Beach, Florida. It is also the first vehicle to utilize a safety belt. Later, he reportedly reaches 127 mph (204 km/h) but without officially being recorded. He later builds an even more powerful vehicle, but he crashes into the crowd at Staten Island Speedway, killing two spectators, and never races again. His 104 mph record stands for 64 years.

1907: Detroit Electric, an electric car produced by the Anderson Electric Car Company, is born. 13,000 Detroit Electrics are produced between 1907 and 1939.

1908: Thomas Edison improves the design of his nickel-iron battery.

1908: Henry Ford starts producing the Model T, but he also buys his wife, Clara, a Detroit Electric Model C coupe (since she preferred electric cars). The Detroit Electric Model C coupe comes with a special baby seat. (The Ford family eventually buys a second Detroit Electric, a Model D, officially sold to Edsel Ford; and then a third one, a Model 47, for Clara.)

1911: The first gasoline-electric hybrid car is released by Woods Motor Vehicle Company, which is based out of Chicago.

1912: 38,843 electric vehicles are on the roads in the United States.

1912: The electric starter is invented by Charles Kettering. Ironically, this harms the electric car market, as gasoline-powered cars can now be easily and quickly started (without having to use a hand crank).

1913: Mass production of the Ford Model T on the first modern assembly line deals a strong blow to early-era electric cars, as it brings down the cost of gasoline cars considerably (making electric cars two or even three times more expensive in the coming years). Electric car sales would slowly taper off over the coming years. (Other main factors leading to the demise of electric cars were: cheap Texas oil; a more developed road network and the ability/desire to travel long distances — electric cars typically had driving ranges of 30 to 40 miles (50 to 65 kilometers) and limited charging infrastructure; the electric starter; slower speeds — about 20 mph or 32 km/h; tough economic times during World War I; and the stigma that electric cars are for women)

1913: With the advent of the self-starter (making it easy for all drivers to start gas engines), steamers and electrics were almost completely wiped out. In this year, sales of electric cars dropped to 6,000 vehicles, while the Ford Model T sold 182,809 gasoline cars.

1923: Milburn, one of few remaining electric vehicle companies, sells out to main body client General Motors.

1929: W.C. Anderson, 75 years old and in poor health, sells his Detroit Electric company. The last entirely new Detroit Electric was likely sold in 1926 anyway.

1957: Sputnik is launched and the US space program engages in advanced battery research & development.

1959-1961: The Henney Kilowatt, a small electric car, is produced by Henney Coachworks and the National Union Electric Company. It achieves a top speed of 60 mph (97 km/h) and a range of 60 miles (97 kilometers), but its high price keeps away potential buyers.

1966: U.S. Congress introduced first bills recommending use of electric vehicles as a means of reducing air pollution.

1967: The Electric Auto Association is founded by Walter Laski.

1967-1969: American Motors Corporation (AMC) & Gulton Industries team up to produce a few electric cars using a lithium-based battery and a nickel-cadmium battery, such as the Amitron (1967, lithium batteries) and and all-electric Rambler American (1969, nickel-cadmium batteries). The Amitron introduces regenerative braking.

1971: The first manned vehicle to drive on the moon, the Lunar Rover, is an electric car.

1972: The Electric Auto Association holds its first annual electric vehicle rally.

1973-1977: The Enfield 8000 (pictured above) is built by Enfield Automotive in the UK. Using lead-acid batteries, the car has a top speed of 48 mph (77 km/h) and a top range of about 40 miles (64 kilometers).

1976: The US Congress passes the Electric and Hybrid Vehicle Research, Development, and Demonstration Act, which increases research and development of electric motors, batteries, and other components of electric and hybrid vehicles.

1977: AMC & Gulton Industries again team up to produce the AMC Electron, a 3-passenger, electric, commuter, city car.

1977–1979: General Motors spent over $20 million in electric car development and research, reporting that electric vehicles could be in production by the mid-1980s.

1983: A fleet of electric vehicles drive from San Jose to San Francisco and back (100 miles / 161 kilometers) without recharging.

1985: Saied Motai drives an electric vehicle 230 miles (370 kilometers) on a single charge.

1990: General Motors (GM) introduces the GM Impact, an electric concept car, at the Los Angeles Auto Show. GM President Roger Smith also announces that GM will produce electric cars for the consumer market (which finally happens in 1997, but the car is only available to lease).

1990: The California Air Resources Board (CARB), the government of California's "clean air agency," pushes for automakers to produce more-fuel-efficient, low-emissions vehicles and eventually transition to zero emissions vehicles (e.g., electric vehicles). The main law is the Zero Emission Vehicle (ZEV) Mandate, which requires 2% of California's vehicles to have 0 tailpipe emissions by 1998, and 10% by 2003. As a result, automakers develop several electric vehicle models in the coming years.

1991: The Kewet, a 100% electric microcar produced in Norway, is introduced.

1992: The Škoda Favorit ELTRA 151L & 151 Pick-Up is released, selling for under $20,000 without subsidy. It has a top speed of 50 mph (80 km/h) and a top range of 50 miles (80 kilometers).

1992: California passes a $1,000 tax credit for electric vehicles.

1994: The GM Impact EV (later named the EV1) drives 187 mph (301 km/h), breaking the electric vehicle speed record. GM also began PrEView, a program whereby 50 handbuilt Impact electric cars would be lent to drivers for periods of 1–2 weeks. This program existed for about 2 years.

1994: The REVA Electric Car Company is formed in India, a joint venture between the Maini Group India and AEV of California.

1996: The first 660 EV1s produced are built with GM lead-acid batteries with an advertised range of 70–100 miles (but closer to 60). (Later, they were upgraded to Panasonic lead-acid batteries and had a realistic driving range of 90 miles. Starting in 1999, 457 Gen2 EV1s had NiMh batteries, with a top range of 160 miles.)

1997: GM releases the Chevrolet S10 EV, an electric pickup truck. It has a top speed of 73 mph (118 km/h) and a top range of 90 miles (144 kilometers). It is produced until 1998.

1997: Honda releases the EV Plus, which has a top speed of over 80 mph (130 km/h) and a top range of 80 to 110 miles (130 to 180 kilometers). It is produced until 1999.

1997: Toyota releases the RAV4 EV, which has a top speed of 78 mph (125 km/h) and a top range of 87 miles (140 kilometers). It is produced until 2002.

1998: Ford releases the Ranger EV, which has a range of 74 miles (119 kilometers). It is produced until 2002.

1999: The Honda Insight and Toyota Prius, hybrid electric cars, go on sale. These are the first hybrid vehicles on the market since the 1917 Woods hybrid. The Insight comes to the US, while the Prius comes to Japan.

2001: REVA Electric Car Company releases the REVAi, an electric microcar powered by lead-acid batteries.

2003: Tesla Motors is founded in California.

2004: Tesla Motors begins work on the Tesla Roadster, a 100% electric sports car based on the design of the popular and stylish Lotus Elise.

2004: The last of the EV1s are taken back from leaseholders and destroyed or donated. All EV1s donated to museums and schools are deactivated, except one. Serial number 660, donated to the Smithsonian, is not disabled.

2010: Nissan's Leaf goes on sale in 2010 and becomes the world's best-selling electric car. Tesla adds more models.

2010: Nissan Leaf all electric car sold. Synchronous electric motor used on front axle.

2011: The Better Place network was the first modern commercial deployment of the battery swapping model. Better Place launched its first battery-swapping station in Israel, in Kiryat Ekron, near Rehovot in March 2011. The Smart electric drive, Wheego Whip LiFe, Mia electric, Volvo C30 Electric, and the Ford Focus Electric were launched for retail customers during 2011.

2012-2013: The next Tesla vehicle, the Model S, was released in the U.S. on 22 June 2012. Other models released to the market in 2012 and 2013 include the BMW ActiveE, Coda, Renault Fluence Z.E., Honda Fit EV, Toyota RAV4

EV, Renault Zoe, Roewe E50, Mahindra e2o, Chevrolet Spark EV, Mercedes-Benz SLS AMG Electric Drive, Fiat 500e, Volkswagen e-Up!, BMW i3, and Kandi EV.

2014: All-electric models released to the retail customers in 2014 include the BMW Brilliance Zinoro 1E, Chery eQ, Geely-Kandi Panda EV, Zotye Zhidou E20, Kia Soul EV, Volkswagen e-Golf, Mercedes-Benz B-Class Electric Drive, and Venucia e30.

2016: The Tesla Model 3 was unveiled on 31 March 2016. The Hyundai Ioniq Electric was released in South Korea in July 2016.

2019: The number of light electric vehicles globally reached 2 264 400 units, 9 % higher than for 2018. This is a clear deviation from the growth rates of the previous 6 years, which were between 46% and 69%.

2020: Another interesting EV trend in 2020 relates to public transportation and the sharing economy. Electric micromobility options have expanded rapidly since their emergence in 2017. Shared electric scooters (e-scooters), electric-assist bicycles (e-bikes) and electric mopeds now available in over 600 cities across more than 50 countries worldwide.

REVIEW QUESTIONS

1. How did the electric car evolve?
2. When was the first electric vehicle invented?
3. Who invented the first electric vehicle?
4. Why did the electric car disappear in the middle?
5. Discuss the evolution of electric vehicle in respect of global scenario.
6. Write a brief history and evolution of electric vehicles in Indian automobile sector.

4 HISTORY OF HYBRID VEHICLES

UNIT OUTCOMES

Upon successful completion of this module, the student will be able to:

1. Study the history of hybrid vehicles.
2. Get exposed to evolution of HEVs.

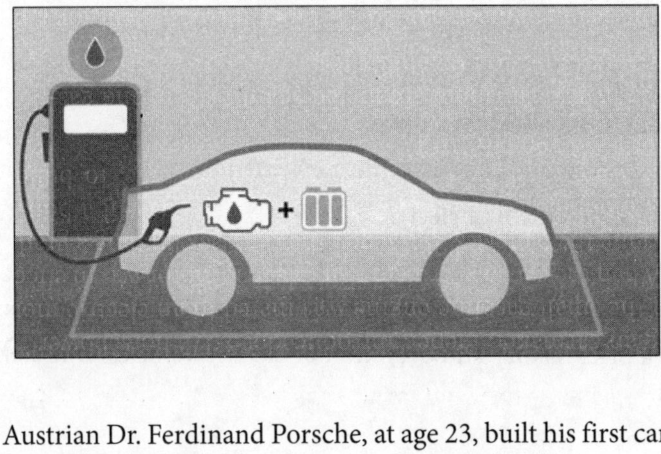

1898: The Austrian Dr. Ferdinand Porsche, at age 23, built his first car, the Lohner Electric Chaise. It was the world's first front-wheel-drive. Porsche's second car was a hybrid, using an internal combustion engine to spin a generator that provided power to electric motors located in the wheel hubs. On battery alone, the car could travel nearly 40 miles.

1899: The Pope Manufacturing Company merged with two smaller electric car companies to form the Electric Vehicle Company, the first large-scale operation in the American automobile industry. The company had assets of $200 million. Two hybrids appeared at the Paris Salon.

1900: A Belgian carmaker, Pieper, introduced a 3-1/2 horsepower "voiturette" in which the small gasoline engine was mated to an electric motor under the seat. When the car was "cruising," its electric motor was in effect a generator, recharging the batteries. But when the car was climbing a grade, the electric motor, mounted coaxially with the gas engine, gave it a boost. The Pieper patents were used by a Belgium firm, Auto-Mixte, to build commercial vehicles from 1906 to 1912.

1902: A series-hybrid runabout competed against steam and gas-powered cars in a New York to Boston reliability test.

1905: An American engineer named H. Piper filed a patent for a petrol-electric hybrid vehicle. His idea was to use an electric motor to assist an internal-combustion engine, enabling it to achieve 25 mph.

1905: The Woods Interurban, an electric car that allowed long-distance drivers to swap the electric power unit for a two-cylinder gas engine (supposedly a fifteen-minute job), failed to get more than a handful of customers.

1910: Commercial built a hybrid truck which used a four-cylinder gas engine to power a generator, eliminating the need for both transmission and battery pack. This hybrid was built in Philadelphia until 1918.

1916: Two prominent electric-vehicle makers-Baker of Cleveland and Woods of Chicago-offered hybrid cars. Woods claimed that their hybrid reached a top speed of 35 mph and achieved fuel efficiency of 48 mpg. The Woods Dual Power was more expensive and less powerful than its gasoline competition, and therefore sold poorly.

1920-1965: Dormant period for mass-produced electric and hybrid cars.

1968-1971: Three scientists working at TRW, a major auto supplier, created a practical hybrid powertrain. Dr. Baruch Berman, Dr. George H. Gelb and Dr. Neal A. Richardson developed, demonstrated and patented the system—designated as an electromechanical transmission (EMT) providing brisk vehicle performance with an engine smaller than required by a conventional internal combustion engine drive. Many of the engineering concepts incorporated in that system are used in today's hybrids.

1969: The GM 512, a very lightweight experimental hybrid car, ran entirely on electric power up to 10 miles per hour. From 10 to 13 miles per hour, it ran on a combination of batteries and its two-cylinder gas engine. Above thirteen miles per hour, the GM 512 ran on gasoline. It could only reach 40 miles per hour.

1970s: With the Arab oil embargo of 1973, the price of gasoline soared, creating new interest in electric vehicles. The U.S. Department of Energy ran tests on many electric and hybrid vehicles produced by various manufacturers, including a hybrid known as the "VW Taxi" produced by Volkswagen in Wolfsburg, West Germany. The Taxi, which used a parallel hybrid configuration allowing flexible switching between the gasoline engine and electric motor, logged over 8,000 miles on the road, and was shown at auto shows throughout Europe and the United States.

1974: As part of the Federal Clean Car Incentive Program, engineers Victor Wouk and Charlie Rosen created a prototype hybrid gas-electric vehicle using a Buick Skylark body. The U.S. Environmental Protection Agency tested the vehicle, certified that it met the strict guidelines for an EPA clean-air auto program-and rejected it out of hand.

1975: AM General, a division of American Motors, began delivery of 352 electric vans to the U.S. Postal Service for testing. The U.S. Energy Research and Development Administration began a government program to advance electric and hybrid technology.

1976: U.S. Congress enacted Public Law 94-413, the Electric and Hybrid Vehicle Research, Development, and Demonstration Act of 1976. Among the law's objectives were to work with industry to improve batteries, motors, controllers, and other hybrid-electric components.

General Electric was chosen to construct a parallel-hybrid sedan, and Toyota built its first hybrid-a small sports car with a gas-turbine generator supplying current to an electric motor.

1979: Dave Arthurs of Springdale, Arkansas, spent $1,500 turning a standard Opel GT into a hybrid car that could get 75 miles per gallon, using a six-horsepower lawnmower engine, a four-hundred-amp electric motor, and an array of six-volt batteries. Mother Earth News used the Arthurs plan to build their own hybrid, which averaged 75 miles per gallon.

1980: Briggs and Stratton, developed a hybrid car powered by a twin cylinder four-stroke 16hp gasoline engine and an electric motor-for total of 26 horsepower. The hybrid drivetrain provided power for a custom-designed two-door vehicle with six wheels-two in front and four in the back.

1989: Audi unveiled the first generation of the Audi Duo experimental vehicle, based on the Audi 100 Avant Quattro. The car had a 12.6 horsepower electric engine, which drove the rear wheels instead of a propeller shaft. A nickel-cadmium battery supplied the energy. The front-wheel drive was powered by a 2.3-litre five-cylinder engine with an output of 136 horsepower. Two years later, Audi unveiled the second generation Duo, also based on the Audi 100 Avant quattro.

1993: The Clinton Administration announced a government initiative called the Partnership for a New Generation of Vehicles (PNGV). In the program, the government worked with the American auto industry to develop a clean car that could operate at up to 80 miles per gallon. Several years and a billion dollars later, the PNGV emerged with three prototypes for their 80 mpg car. Every prototype was a hybrid.

1997: The Toyota Prius was introduced to the Japanese market, two years before its original launch date, and prior to the Kyoto global warming conference held in December. First-year sales were nearly 18,000.

1997: Audi became the first manufacturer in Europe to take a hybrid vehicle into volume production: the Audi duo based on the A4 Avant. The vehicle was powered by a 90 horsepower 1.9-litre TDI in conjunction with a 29 horsepower electric motor. Both power sources drove the front wheels. A lead-gel battery at the rear stored the electrical energy. The Duo was not a commercial success and therefore discontinued, prompting European carmakers to focus their R&D investment on diesels.

1997-1999: A small selection of all-electric cars from the big automakers-including Honda's EV Plus, GM's EV1 and S-10 electric pickup, a Ford Ranger pickup, and Toyota's RAV4 EV-were introduced in California. Despite the enthusiasm of early adopters, the electrics failed to reach beyond a few hundred drivers for each model. Within a few years, the all-electric programs were dropped.

1999: Honda released the two-door Insight, the first hybrid car to hit the mass market in the United States. The Insight won numerous awards and received EPA mileage ratings of 61 mpg city and 70 mpg highway.

2000: Toyota released the Toyota Prius, the first hybrid four-door sedan available in the United States.

2002: Honda introduced the Honda Civic Hybrid, its second commercially available hybrid gasoline-electric car. The appearance and drivability of the Civic Hybrid was (and still is) identical to the conventional Civic.

2004: The Toyota Prius II won 2004 Car of the Year Awards from Motor Trend Magazine and the North American Auto Show. Toyota was surprised by the demand and pumped up its production from 36,000 to 47,000 for the U.S. market. Interested buyers waited up to six months to purchase the 2004 Prius. Toyota Motor Sales U.S.A. President Jim Press called it "the hottest car we've ever had." In September, Ford released the Escape Hybrid, the first American hybrid and the first SUV hybrid.

2008: Tesla Motors sells the Tesla Roadster with a 200+ mile range

2009: Ford Fusion hybrid is released.

2010: Mercedes-Benz collaborates with Tesla Motor Company to produce the A-Class E-Cell.

2011: Chevy Volt, hybrid car, sold in US market with a 25-50 mile range.

2012: Toyota announced the launching of RAV4 Hybrid as 2012 model in the spring of 2012. The Peugeot 3008 HYbrid4 was launched in the European market in 2012, becoming the world's first production diesel-electric hybrid.

2013: The Range Rover Hybrid diesel-powered electric hybrid was unveiled at the 2013 Frankfurt Motor Show, and retail deliveries in Europe are slated to start in early 2014.

2014: Honda introduced its own two-motor hybrid system on the 2014 Accord. The first production micro-hybrid system4 is Mazda's i-ELOOP, which the company introduced in 2014 on the Mazda3 and Mazda6.

2015: The redesigned and more efficient fourth generation Prius was released for retail customers in Japan in December 2015.

2020: As of April 2020, more than 17 million hybrid electric vehicles have been sold worldwide since their inception in 1997. Japan ranks as the market leader with more than 7.5 million hybrids sold as of March 2018.

REVIEW QUESTIONS

1. When was the first hybrid electric vehicle invented?
2. Who invented the first hybrid electric vehicle?
3. Discuss the evolution of hybrid electric vehicle in respect of global scenario.
4. Write a brief history and evolution of hybrid electric vehicles in Indian automobile sector.

5 ELECTRIC VEHICLE

UNIT OUTCOMES

Upon successful completion of this module, the student will be able to:

1. Study the sources of electricity for EVs.
2. Identify the major components of EVs
3. Get exposed to problems of EVs.
4. Apply the energy management system in EVs

ELECTRIC VEHICLES

Electric vehicles are defined as vehicles which use an electric motor for propulsion. Electric vehicle is propelled by one or more electric motors, receiving power from an onboard source of electricity such as batteries, fuel cells, ultracapacior, flywheel, etc.

When the car pedal is pressed, then:

- Controller takes and regulates electrical energy from batteries and inverters.
- With the controller set, the inverter then sends a certain amount of electrical energy to the motor (according to the depth of pressure on the pedal).
- Electric motor converts electrical energy into mechanical energy (rotation).
- Rotation of the motor rotor rotates the transmission so the wheels turn and then the car moves.

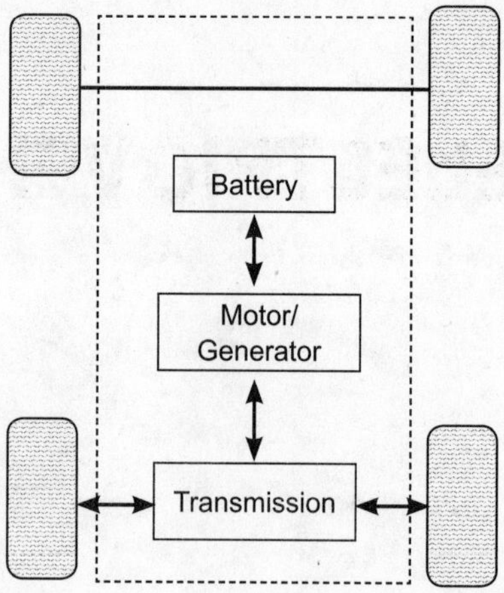

Fig. 5.1: Layout of an electric vehicle

EVs include a large range of vehicles from electric two-wheelers, three-wheelers (rickshaws), cars and electric buses and trucks.

NEED FOR ELECTRIC VEHICLE

The main reasons for the need of electric vehicles are:

- Depletion of oil reserves
- Stringent emission standards
- Noise pollution

There would be no exhaust emissions emitted from electric drives. This zero emission vehicles are almost noiseless and can be charged at home or work place. EVs are easier to service and maintain due to the absence of spark plugs, clutch and gears. They are ideal for 'stop-start' city driving conditions. EVs are extremely reliable and ease to drive.

It is known that almost any fuel can be used to generate electricity. Therefore our dependence upon petroleum can be reduced by switching to electric vehicles.

ADVANTAGES OF ELECTRIC VEHICLE

1. Mechanically simpler.
2. Running cost per kilometre is extremely cheap.
3. Zero emission vehicle. Also reducing greenhouse emission
4. They are very quiet in operation. While running, it does not produce noise and vibrations.
5. Easy to drive as there are no gears and clutch in these vehicles.

6. Minimum maintenance and serviceas EVs have fewer moving parts.
7. Ideal for stop-start city driving conditions.
8. More durable than gasoline-powered cars.
9. More energy efficient than gasoline engines.
10. Reduce dependency on imported energy sources.
11. Power regeneration.

DISADVANTAGES OF ELECTRIC VEHICLE

1. Vehicle range is limited on one charge. The vehicle can usually run 80-160 km on a single charge.
2. Top speed is limited.
3. It is heavy and bulky.
4. Limited public charging stations.

MAJOR COMPONENTS OF ELECTRIC VEHICLE

An electric vehicle consists of a battery that provides energy, an electric motor that drives the wheels, a charger that charges the battery and a controller that regulates the energy flow to the motor. There are no gearbox and clutch in these vehicles.

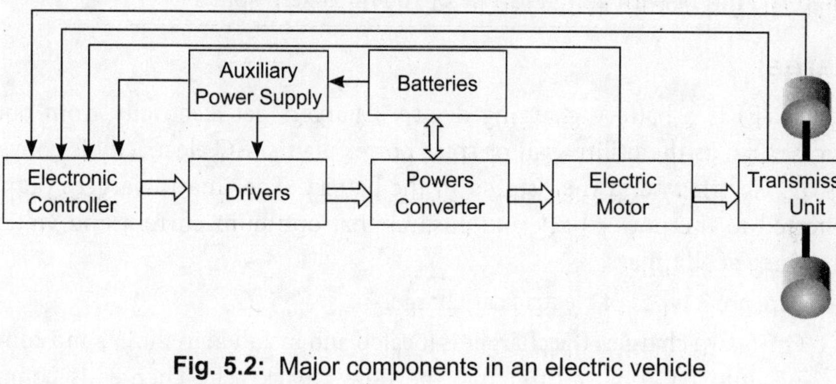

Fig. 5.2: Major components in an electric vehicle

Power pack (Battery)

Automobile manufacturers use three types of rechargeable battery for electric car use. Those types are lead-acid batteries, nickel metal hydride (NiMH) batteries, and lithium-ion (Li-ion) batteries. The space occupied by these heavy batteries is large. Operational problems include the limited range of the vehicle and its comparatively low maximum speed. Currently the main advantage of lead-acid batteries is the existing mature technology, which is accepted by the motor industry.

Taking REVA (India's first zero polluting vehicle for city mobility) as an example, REVA's Power Pack consists of eight 6-Volt EV tubular type lead acid batteries that attain 80 percent state of charge (quick-charge mode) in under 2.5 hours. A complete charge is achieved in less than seven hours and gives a range of 80 km. The power pack is housed beneath the front seats, which lowers the center of gravity, thus increasing the safety of passengers. Charging REVA is a safe and easy process - just plug into a 220 Volt, 15 Ampere socket at home or at work. A full charge consumes just about 9 units of electricity.

Motor

The prime mover in electric vehicle is the high-torque electric motor. The motor converts the energy stored in the power pack into mechanical motion. The high torque electric motor ensures a quick acceleration. The power from the motor is delivered to the wheels directly or through the transaxle that propels the vehicle. While braking, the motor acts like a generator (regenerative braking) and recharges the batteries.

There are several choices of the type of drive motor. The basic choice is between an AC and a DC motor. The AC motor offers many control advantages but requires the DC produced by the batteries to be converted using an inverter. A DC shunt wound motor rated at about 50 kW is a popular choice for the smaller vehicles but AC motors are likely to become the most popular. REVA has a 13 kW separately excited DC motor with a high torque of 70 Nm at zero speed.

Charger

Charger (E) is a battery charging device. Chargers get electricity from outside sources, such as the utility grid or solar power plants. AC electricity is converted into DC electricity and then stored in the battery. The smart charger's output is connected to the power pack and ensures that optimum current and voltage is maintained at all times.

There are 2 types of electric car chargers:

- On-board charger: the charger is located and installed in the car and converts AC into DC power to charge the power pack. The charger is computer controlled with an in-built stabilizer and auto shut-off mechanism.
- Off-board charger: the charger is not located or not installed in the car.

Controller

EVs have a computerised motor controller. The electric vehicle controller is the electronics package that operates between the batteries and the motor to control the electric vehicle's speed and acceleration much like a carburettor does in a gasoline-powered vehicles. This regulates the flow of energy from the power pack to the motor in direct relation to pressure applied on the accelerator. It ensures perfect speed control and optimum use of energy in both forward and reverse directions. Speed controllers are rated according to the voltage and amperage ranges.

DC/DC converter

The DC/DC converter changes DC power from an on-board 200-800V high voltage battery into lower DC voltage (13.5, charging voltage) to recharge the auxiliary battery. A 12 V auxiliary battery is normally used in an electric car to power all 12 V accessories such as lights, wiper and window motors, pumps horn and so on. There is no alternator in EVs to keep this battery charged. EVs use a DC/DC converter which taps the full battery pack voltage and cuts it down to a regulated 13.5 V output, similar to an alternator. It is not advisable to eliminate the auxiliary battery completely, for safety reasons. If the DC/DC converter fails at night or the battery pack falls below the low voltage shut-off of the converter, the auxiliary battery will have enough charge to bring the car home.

Energy Management System (EMS)

The brain of EVs is the Energy Management System (EMS) that monitors and controls all required functions. The EMS is a computer-based system that optimises charging and energy output of batteries to maximise operating range and improve performance. The EMS increases the electric vehicle range by 10-15% and battery life by 25-30%.

The system also predicts available range for a given state of battery charge. The EMS also maintains an electronic log of the vehicle performance, enables service personnel to run diagnostic checks on the car to give service information about the car.

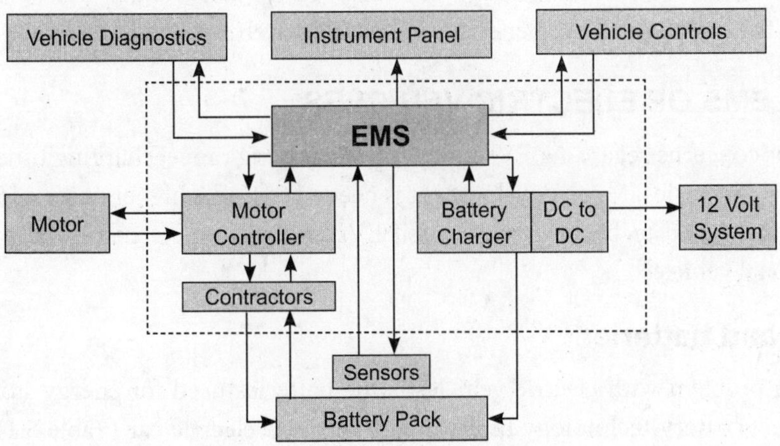

Fig. 5.3 Energy management system

Compared with Internal Combustion Engine Vehicles (ICEVs), EVs offer a relatively short driving range. Thus, in order to maximize the utilization of on-board stored energy, an intelligent energy management system (EMS) needs to be adopted. Making use of sensory inputs from various EV subsystems, including sensors for temperatures of outside and inside air, current and voltage of the energy source during charging and discharging,current and voltage of the electric motor, vehicle speed and acceleration as well as external climate and environment, the EMS can realise the following functions:

- Optimize the system energy flow
- Predict the remaining available energy and hence the residual driving range
- Suggest more efficient driving behaviour.
- Direct regenerative energy from braking to receptive energy sources such as batteries
- Modulate temperature control in response to external climate
- Adjust lighting brightness in response to external environment
- Propose a suitable battery charging algorithm
- Analyse the operation history of the energy source, especially the battery
- Diagnose any incorrect operation or defective components of the energy source.

When the EMS is coupled with a navigation system, it can plan energy efficient routes, locate charging facilities for extended trips, and modify range predictions on the basis of traffic conditions. In summary, the EMS has the distinct features of integrated multi-functions, flexibility and adaptability (just like the brain of EVs) such that the limited on-board energy can be used wisely.

PROBLEMS OF ELECTRIC VEHICLES

The major concerns regarding EVs today is their driving range, charging time and efficiency of batteries. Much development is needed to find a higher energy, longer lasting battery, and to bring down costs if EVs are to compete successfully with conventional vehicles.

Range and batteries

The main problem with electric vehicles is the batteries used for energy storage. The current battery technology limits the distance an electric car (Table 5.1) can travel before its battery must be recharged. The average driving range of electric vehicles has been increasing steadily. The average range for the new battery EVs in

2020 is around 350 km, compared to 200 km in 2015 on the order of one-fifth of what can be easily realized with a gasoline engine powered vehicle.

In this case, the customers are forced to rely on the public charging points. Although the number of charging stations is increasing, it is still incomparable with the convenience of the petrol stations and their density. And accessories, such as air-conditioning or music system, drain the battery even more quickly. Batteries have about 1% of the energy per unit mass of a typical automotive fuel, and a life span of about 2-3 years. Batteries typically account for one-third or more of the vehicle weight. High capital cost of batteries is also a drawback.

A breakthrough in battery technology is required if electric vehicles are to become a significant part of the automotive transportation.

Table 5.1: Approximate range for EVs on the market

EV model	Apprx. range on full charge
Tesla Model S	500km
Nissan Leaf	151km
BMW i3	190km - petrol range extender option available
Kia Soul	148km
Honda Fit	132km
Chevrolet Spark	132km
Ford Focus Electric	122km
BEV Electron	120km
Mitsubishi i-Miev	150km
Mitsubishi Outlander	50km electric only with the back-up of a 45 litre petrol engine

Charging time

A majority of the EV owners (95%) usually charge their cars' batteries during the night, when they are not using the car. Charging at night when consumption is low, allows for efficient use of electricity. Anyway, not all the members of the population have the facility of parking in a garage. Many people park their cars in the street.

To charge the battery fully it takes about 6-7 hrs. The charging time is another issue, as charging time on the stations compared to refuelling diesel/petrol is high. This issue can be solved with the so-called rapid chargers, adding to the vehicle's range within less than an hour.

As battery types and battery technologies improve, the concerns regarding driving range and charging time will get further reduced.

Infrastructure for charging

The infrastructure support for electric vehicles should be provided by the country for them to be convenient. This mainly leads to the charging points that are to be very essentials for EVs. Right now electric vehicles practically cannot be used on highways as there are no charging points across highways or in the countries.

Lack of performance

Electric cars are not able to accelerate, cruise, and climb fast enough when compared to gasoline-powered cars.

Purchase price

The purchase price of any electric car is generally much higher than any other conventional vehicle from given class and quality segment. The main reason for electric cars being so expensive is mainly their battery price.

Safety and reliability

The general perception among people is that EVs are not safe. Present EVs incorporate many safety features like the steel space frame, side impact beams, dent-proof ABS body panels, low voltage system, and dual braking system. All these features lead to a very high level of reliability and safety. Today all EVs are safer than any of the conventional vehicles available on the road.

Fear of running out of charge in the middle of the road

Many customers have this fear that without proper warning the car will run out of charge leaving them stranded. To counter this EVs incorporates a number of warnings to ensure that the customer gets ample warning signals in the form of a warning display on the instrument panel.

Service of electric vehicles

Trained mechanics are not yet developed for these kinds of vehicles. EVs will only lead to causing more problems in this area.

One cannot just call a normal mechanic like people would for a normal vehicle. They will have to call some company authorized service personnel only. There is a general lack of awareness about EVs and their mechanical systems. Therefore, until a substantial amount of them are not there on the road, most of the mechanics would not know about their complete systems, and therefore it will lead to causing inconvenience for the consumer.

REVIEW QUESTIONS

1. When was the first electric car made?
2. What's the Lifespan of an Electric Car Battery?
3. Why are Electric Cars so Expensive?
4. How long does it take to charge an EV?
5. What is the range of an EV?

6. Are electric cars expensive to run?
7. Do electric cars have transmissions?
8. How much does it cost to charge an electric car?
9. How do I charge an electric car?
10. Are electric cars better for the environment?
11. How long do electric cars last?
12. What are the classifications of an electric vehicle EV?
13. How do you classify EVs on the basis of charging time?
14. What are the four types of electric vehicles?
15. What are the types of electric vehicles?
16. How do you classify EVs on the basis of driving range?
17. How do you classify EVs on the basis of driving arrangement?
18. What is the range of maximum distance an EV can run when fully charged?

6 CLASSIFICATION OF EVs

UNIT OUTCOMES

Upon successful completion of this module, the student will be able to:

1. Study the sources of propulsion for HEVs.
2. Identify the major components of HEVs
3. Get exposed to problems of HEVs.
4. Apply the energy management system in HEVs

EVs can be classified on the basis of their attributes such as (i) charging time, (ii) driving range, and (iii) the drive arrangement.

CHARGING TIME (time required to fully charge the battery)

A measure of the time taken to charge the battery to 100% from 0%. Charging time depends on the input power characteristics (i.e. input voltage and current), battery type, and battery capacity. The charging time is typically less than 8 hours, but for some vehicles the charging time tends to be higher.

The charging of an electric vehicle can be classified according to the charging time: conventional, semi-fast and fast.

Conventional charging (16 amps)

In conventional charging, the electric vehicle is plugged into a common outlet for approximately 8 hours to fully charge it. This charging type uses the same electric intensity and voltage of a house, which is 16 amps and 230 VAC (volts alternating current). Therefore, it is ideal if the vehicle is charged in the garage during the night.

Semi-fast charging (32 amps)

With this type of charging, the electric vehicle's battery needs only 4 hours to fully charge. It uses 32 amps and 230 VAC , which implies an electric power of approximately 7.3 kW (kilowatt).

Fast charging

In fast charging, the vehicle needs only about 30 minutes to charge 80% of its battery. When using a higher electric intensity, fast charging delivers energy in direct current and obtains an output power of about 50 kW. It requires special infrastructure and is conceived as a solution to increase electric vehicles' range or as a convenient charge.

DRIVING RANGE (maximum distance an EV can run when fully charged)

A measure of the distance electric vehicles can cover on a single charge of battery. The driving range of EVs could be as low as 20 km per charge to as high as 400 km per charge.

There are 3 types of electric vehicles according to the driving range and source of power: Battery Electric Vehicle (BEV), Hybrid Electric Vehicle (HEV), and Plugin Hybrid Electric Vehicle (PHEV) and each are described in more detail below.

Battery Electric Vehicle (BEV)

In a fully electric car (BEV), there is no engine (internal combustion engine). A BEV runs entirely using an electric motor and battery, without the support of a traditional internal combustion engine, and must be plugged into an external source of electricity to recharge its battery. Like all electric vehicles, BEVs can also recharge their batteries through a process known as regenerative braking, which uses the vehicle's electric motor to assist in slowing the vehicle, and to recover some of the energy normally converted to heat by the brakes. Fig. 6.1 shows basic configuration for BEVs in which the wheels are driven by electric motor(s) which is run by batteries through a controller circuit.

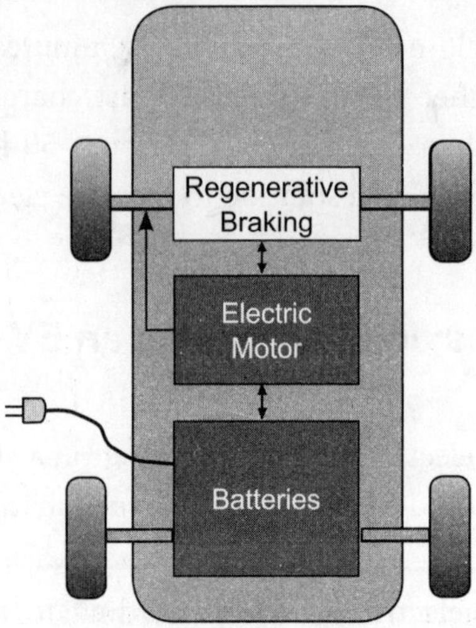

Fig. 6.1 Basic configuration for BEVs

BEVs have to rely solely on the energy stored in their battery packs. Therefore the range of such vehicles depends directly on the battery capacity. Typically they can cover 100 km - 250 km on one charge, whereas the top-tier models can go a lot further, from 300 km to 500 km. These ranges depend on driving condition and style, vehicle configurations, road conditions, climate, battery type and age. Once depleted, charging the battery pack takes quite a lot of time compared to refueling a conventional internal combustion engine vehicle. Charging time depends on the charger configuration, its infrastructure and operating power level.

Vehicle model	Range	Charge time
Tesla Model S	335 – 426 km	5 hours
Nissan Leaf	120 km	3 hours
BMW i3	160 km	6 hours
Mitsubishi iMi	100 km	7 hours
Smart	109 km	6 hours
Ford Focus	110 km	4 hours

Charging

The battery of BEV is charged through an external source of power such as DC fast charger or AC charger. On average, the BEVs take around 8 hours to get fully charged by an AC charger. This time can be reduced to 1 hour using a DC fast charger.

Range

These electric vehicles have a range from 250 kms to 500 kms depending upon the battery capacity and the motor.

Advantages

- No emissions while running
- Silent
- No gas or oil changes
- Ability to conveniently charge at home
- Fast and smooth acceleration
- Low cost of operation
- Instant and high torques, even at low speeds

Disadvantages

- Shorter range than gasoline vehicles.
- More expensive than their gasoline equivalent.

Application

Nissan Leaf and Teslas are some high-selling BEVs these days, along with some Chinese vehicles. Some of the 4-wheeler BEVs in India are Tata Nexon EV, Hyundai Kona Electric, Mahindra eKUV100, MG ZS EV, etc. 2-wheeler BEVs in India include Ather 450, TVS iQube, Bajaj Chetak Electric, etc.

Hybrid Electric Vehicle (HEV)

These type of electric vehicles are powered by both, fuel as well as electricity. The electric motor is used to start off the HEVs. Then the propulsion is taken care of by the IC engine. This ensures better fuel economy. The operation of the engine as well as the motor is controlled by the ECU.

Hybrid Electric Vehicles (HEVs) produce supplemental fuel source to produce electricity on-board. HEVs have two complementary drive systems: an engine with a fuel tank and an electric motor with a battery. Both the engine and the electric motor can turn the transmission at the same time, and the transmission then turns the wheels. HEVs need not be recharged from the electricity grid – all their energy comes from gasoline and from regenerative braking. Fig. 6.2 shows basic configuration for HEVs the wheels are driven by both electric motor(s) and internal combustion engine through a controller circuit.

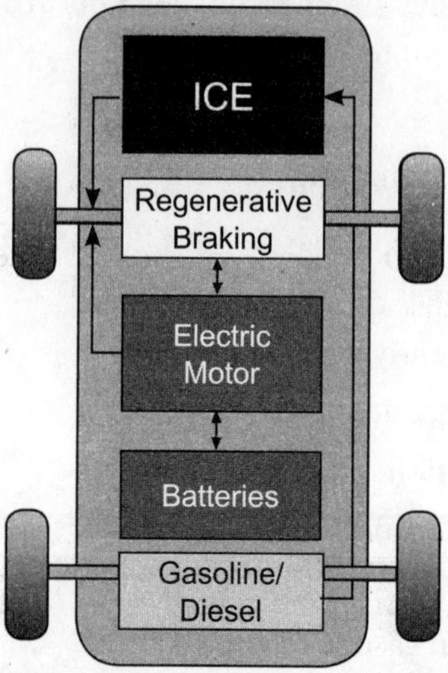

Fig. 6.2: Basic configuration for HEVs

An HEV uses the electric propulsion system when the power demand is low. It is a great advantage in low speed conditions like urban areas. It also reduces the fuel consumption as the engine stays totally off during idling periods, for example, traffic jams. This feature also reduces the greenhouse gas emission. When higher speed is needed, the HEV switches to the engine mode. The two drive trains can also work together to improve the performance.

Vehicle model	Range	Charge time
Audi Q5 Hybrid	NA	NA
BMW Active Hybrid	NA	NA
Honda Civic Hybrid	NA	NA
Hyundai Sonata Hybrid	NA	NA

Hybrid power systems are used extensively to reduce or to completely remove turbo lag in turbocharged cars, like the Acura NSX. It also enhances performance by filling the gaps between gear shifts and providing speed boosts when required. The internal combustion engine can charge up the batteries. HEVs can also retrieve energy by means of regenerative braking. Therefore, HEVs are primarily engine driven cars that use an electrical drive train to improve mileage or for performance enhancement. To attain these features, HEV configurations are being widely adopted by car manufacturers.

A typical hybrid electric vehicle is fuelled by gasoline and uses a battery-powered motor to improve efficiency, thus is not considered a plug-in electric vehicle. The battery in a gasoline hybrid is never plugged into an electrical outlet, but instead is powered by a combination of the gasoline engine and regenerative braking.

Advantages

1. Low exhaust emission levels than internal combustion engines.
2. Increased range compared to electric vehicles.
3. Engines can be down sized to accommodate average load, not peak load, which reduces the engine's weight.
4. Fuel efficiency is greatly increased.
5. Emissions are greatly decreased.

Disadvantages

1. Bulky and heavy.
2. Require very complicated control systems.
3. Cost is very high.

Application

The most well known HEV is the Toyota Prius. Some HEVs in India are Toyota Prius hybrid, Honda Civic hybrid and Toyota Camry hybrid. Maruti Suzuki recently introduced its hybrid system in few models too.

Plug-In Hybrid Electric Vehicle (PHEV)

These are types of HEVs which can recharge the bateries through regenerative battery or through the external source of power. Plug-in hybrid vehicles (PHEVs) use an electric motor and battery that can be plugged into the power grid to charge the battery, but also have the support of an internal combustion engine that may be used to recharge the vehicle's battery and/or to replace the electric motor when the battery is low. Because Plug-in Hybrids use electricity from the power grid, they often realise more savings in fuel costs than traditional HEVs.

Range

The HEVs travel about 3-4 kms before the engine is switch on. PHEVs can go up to 65 kms before the engine provide the required assistance for the propulsion of the vehicle.

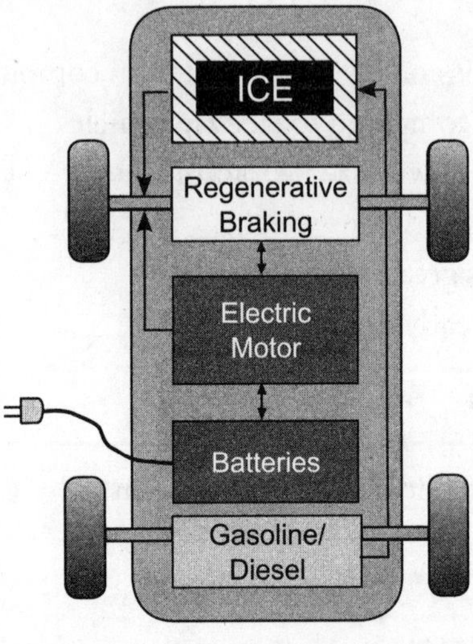

Fig. 6.3: Plug-in hybrid electric vehicle

Vehicle model	Range	Charge time
BMW i3	160 km on electric, 160 on petrol	6 hours
Cadillac ELR	59 km on electric, 488 km on petrol	2 hours
GM Chevy Volt	60 km on electric, 500 km on petrol	2 hours
Ford Fusion Energi	42 km on electric, 940 km on petrol	2-3 hours
Toyota Prius Plug-in	50 km on electric, 785 km on petrol	1-2 hours

These vehicles generally run on the electric motor until the battery is depleted, at which point the engine can kick in, extending the car's range.

Advantages

1. Longer range than BEV
2. Less gas consumption than gas only vehicle
3. Fewer emissions
4. Very simple mechanics, less to go wrong.

Disadvantages

1. Produces tailpipe emissions
2. Needs fuel and oil changes
3. More expensive to operate than BEV but less than traditional HEV.

Application

An example of a plug-in hybrid is the Chevrolet Volt. PHEV option available in India are Mahindra e-Verito, BMW i8, and the Volvo XC90 T8.

DRIVE ARRANGEMENT

Conventional type

Conventional type uses traditional transmission (gearbox) in the drivetrain system of an electric vehicle.

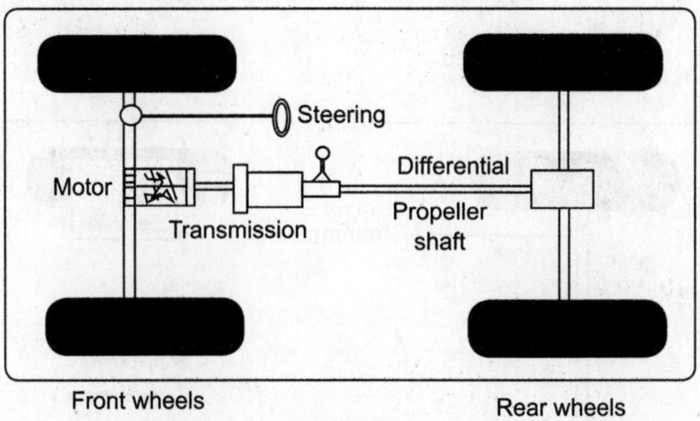

Fig. 6.4: Conventional type

No-transmission type

In a no-transmission type, there is no conventional gearbox. Motor torque is transmitted to the wheels through propeller shaft and differential assembly.

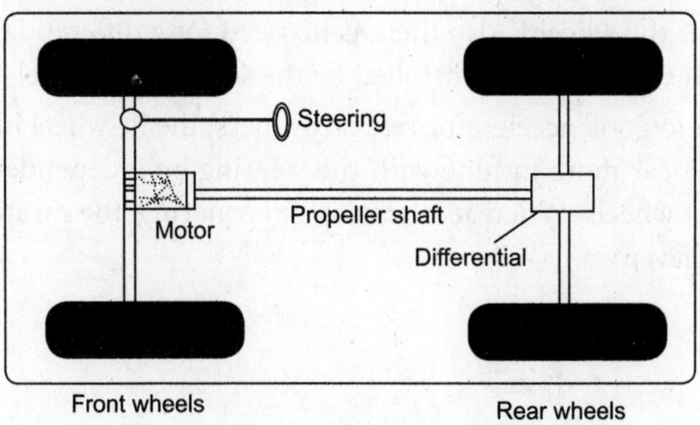

Fig. 6.5: No-transmission type

No differential type

Each wheel has an individual motor and hence differential is not required.

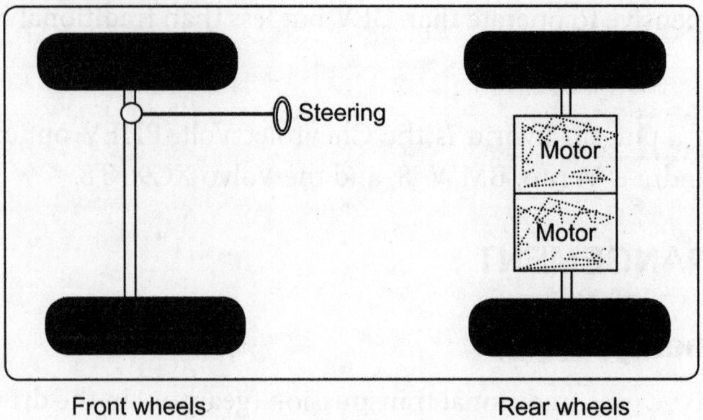

Fig. 6.6: No differential type

In-wheel motor type

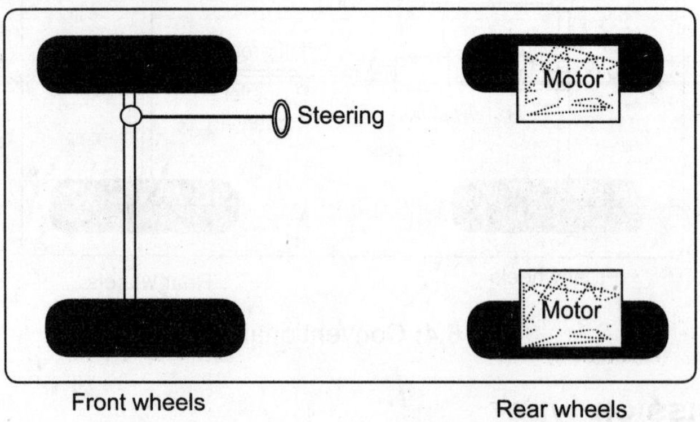

Fig. 6.7: In-wheel motor type

The in-wheel motor EV installs motors right around each of the driving wheels to directly power the wheels. Also there is no need for a differential as the amount of power to each wheel can be controlled by the separate in-wheel electric motors.

In addition to good accelerator responsiveness, the in-wheel motor makes the behaviour of the car more in tune with the steering by independently controlling the left and right wheels. When accelerating or cornering, the car moves intuitively in the way the driver wants.

REVIEW QUESTIONS

1. What are the two main types of hybrid vehicles?
2. What is the difference between a plug in hybrid and battery electric vehicle?
3. What are the two main types of hybrid vehicle?
4. What are the important subsystems in an electric hybrid vehicle?
5. What are the main components of hybrid electric vehicle?
6. What is the advantage of a hybrid vehicle?
7. What is the most common form of hybrid energy vehicle?
8. What makes hybrid electric vehicles special?

7 ENERGY SOURCES

UNIT OUTCOMES

Upon successful completion of this module, the student will be able to:

1. Study the requirements of EVs energy sources
2. Study the sources of electricity for EVs.
3. Identify the major types of batteries for EVs
4. Get exposed to parameters that affect the performance of a battery.
5. Identify the alternative energy storage devices.

EVs can get the energy required to run from different sources. EVs use different types of energy storage to store their power. They include:

- Batteries
- Ultra capacitors
- Flywheels
- Fuel cells

Requirements of EVs Energy Sources

The criteria such sources have to satisfy are:

1. High specific energy and energy density
2. High specific power and power density
3. Fast charging and deep discharging capabilities
4. Long cycle and service life
5. Low self discharging rate and high charging efficiency
6. Safety and cost effectiveness
7. Maintenance free
8. Environmentally sound and recyclable

High specific energy is required from a source to provide a long driving range whereas high specific power helps to increase the acceleration. The other characteristics that make a perfect energy source are fast charging, long service and cycle life, less cost and maintenance.

BATTERY

Batteries have been the major energy source for EVs for a long time. The battery converts stored chemical energy into electric energy. The chemical reaction between the electrodes and electrolyte generates electricity. Rechargeable batteries can reverse the chemical reaction by reversing the current. This way the battery can be recharged.

Battery is the most important component of an electric vehicle and typically constitutes up to about half of the vehicle cost and weight. The choice of batteries depends on the energy density, weight and costs.

The range of an electric vehicle is determined by the amount of energy at disposal in the battery and the energy consumption of the vehicle. The available total energy in the batteries for vehicles is called the battery capacity and the remaining amount of energy during use is called the state of charge (SoC) and is expressed in percentage "charge" remaining.

Electric cycles and low range mopeds have simple battery units while electric cars deploy a large number of batteries.

Requirement of EV batteries

The batteries should have

1. A stable voltage output over a good depth of discharge
2. High energy capacity for the given battery weight and size
3. High peak power output per unit mass and volume
4. High energy efficiency
5. Able to function with wide ranges of operating temperatures
6. Good charge retention on open-circuit stand
7. Ability to accept fast recharge
8. Ability to withstand overcharge and over discharge
9. Reliable in operation
10. Maintenance free
11. Rugged and resistant to abuse
12. Safe both in use and accident conditions

13. Made of readily available and inexpensive materials with environmental friendliness
14. Efficient reclamation of materials at the end of service life

Selection of Battery

This depends on mainly the voltage. The higher the voltage, the better the acceleration, and a higher top speed can be achieved. A normal sized EV using a voltage system of 96-120V with 6 deep-cycle batteries will give more amphere hours and weigh more. Therefore, it will have a fairly high range but poor performance. The same vehicle using a voltage system of 96-120 with 12V batteries will give high performance, but lower range. That is because the battery pack will be lighter and in turn the vehicle will be lighter.

Deep-cycle batteries

Deep-cycle batteries are normally available in three voltage sizes: 6, 8 and 12V. For range, 6V batteries are used because of their high specific energy. For performance, 12 V batteries are used. The 8 V battery packs offer a good balance between the range of the 6V battery and the acceleration capabilities of the 12V battery.

TYPES OF BATTERY FOR EVs

The following types of batteries are commonly used today in EVs: (1) Lead-acid, (2) Nickel-cadmium (NiCd), (3) Nickel-Metal Hydride (NiMH), (4) Lithium-ion (Li-ion), (5) ZEBRA batteries. Traditionally, most electric vehicles used lead-acid batteries due to their mature technology, easy availability, and low cost. More recently, batteries using combinations of Li-ion and its variations are gaining widespread acceptance due to better efficiency, reduced weight, lower charging time, better power output, longer lifetime, and reduced environmental implications from battery disposal.

The comparison of the four types of electric car batteries can be seen as follows:

Table 7.1: Comparison of different types of EV batteries

Understanding Electric Car Batteries				
	Lithium Ion	Nickel-Metal	Lead-Acid	Ultracapacitors
Easy Access/ Inexpensive	✓	✗	✓	✗
Energy Efficient	✓	✓	✓	✓

Understanding Electric Car Batteries				
	Lithium Ion	Nickel-Metal	Lead-Acid	Ultracapacitors
Temperature performance	✓	✗	✗	✓
Reduced weight	✓	✓	✓	✓
Life Cycle	✓	✗	✓	✗

LEAD-ACID BATTERY

Lead-acid batteries are the oldest rechargeable batteries. Compared to lithium and NiMH batteries, lead-acid batteries do lose capacity and are much heavier, but the price is relatively cheap and safe. There are large capacity lead-acid electric car batteries under development, but lead-acid batteries are now only used by commercial vehicles as a secondary storage system.

It is called lead-acid battery because its active ingredients are the metal lead and sulphuric acid. The difference in voltage between the positive plate (lead peroxide) and the negative plate (spongy lead) is 2.13 V when a sulphuric acid solution of 1.265 – 1.280 specific gravity is added, and the temperature is 68°F-80°F. Lead peroxide and spongy lead are used in the automotive battery today because no other materials have a greater voltage difference.

1. Chemical reaction when discharging

$$\underset{\text{(+ plate)}}{PbO_2} + \underset{\text{(electrolyte)}}{2H_2SO_4} + \underset{\text{(– plate)}}{Pb} \longrightarrow \underset{\text{(+ plate)}}{PbSO_4} + \underset{\text{(water)}}{2H_2O} + \underset{\text{(– plate)}}{PbSO_4}$$

2. Chemical reaction when charging

$$\underset{\text{(+ plate)}}{PbSO_4} + \underset{\text{(water)}}{2H_2O} + \underset{\text{(– plate)}}{PbSO_4} \longrightarrow \underset{\text{(+ plate)}}{PbSO_4} + \underset{\text{(electrolyte)}}{2H_2SO_4} + \underset{\text{(– plate)}}{Pb}$$

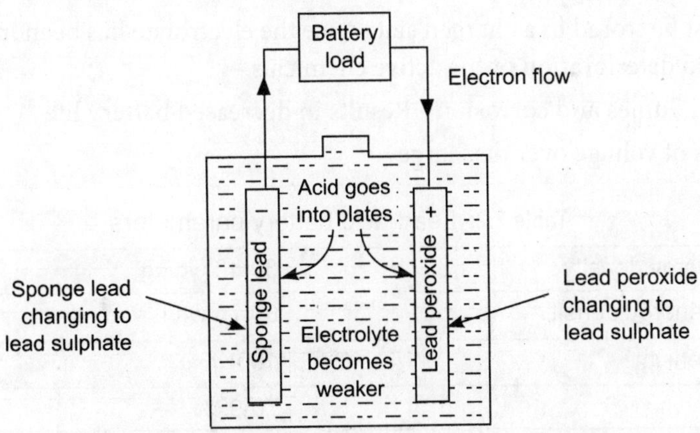

Fig. 7.1: Discharging of a lead-acid battery

Discharge

During discharge, the lead dioxide (positive plate) and lead (negative plate) react with the electrolyte of sulphuric acid to create lead sulfate, water and energy.

Charge

During charging, the cycle is reversed: the lead sulphate and water are electrochemically converted to lead, lead oxide and sulphuric acid by an external electrical charging source.

Advantages

1. Reliable
2. Robust
3. Better range
4. Rapid recharge
5. Tolerant to overcharging
6. Low internal impedance
7. Can deliver very high currents
8. Ability to hold charge over a period of not being used
9. Indefinite shelf life if stored without electrolyte
10. Can be left on trickle or float charge for prolonged periods
11. Wide range of sizes and capacities available

Disadvantages

1. Heavy and bulky
2. Very low specific energy
3. Danger of overheating during charging
4. Not suitable for fast charging
5. Typical cycle life 300 to 500 cycles
6. Must be stored in a charged state once the electrolyte has been introduced to avoid deterioration of the active chemicals
7. Acid Fumes and corrosion - Results in decreased battery life
8. Loss of voltage over discharge

Table 7.2: Lead-acid battery parameters

Mass energy density	30-40 wh/kg
Volume energy density	60-75 wh/L
Power density	180 w/kg
Efficiency	70-92%
Self-discharge rate	3-20% / month

Cycle durability	500-800 cycles
Typical cost	₹12-23 / wh

NICKEL-CADMIUM BATTERY

Lead-acid batteries require a considerable amount of servicing to keep them in good condition, although this is not applicable with sealed and maintenance-free batteries. However, when a battery is required to withstand a high rate of charge and discharge on a regular basis, or is left in a state of discharge for long periods, the lead-acid cell is not ideal. Alkaline cells on the other hand require minimum maintenance and are able to withstand heavy discharge and over-charging.

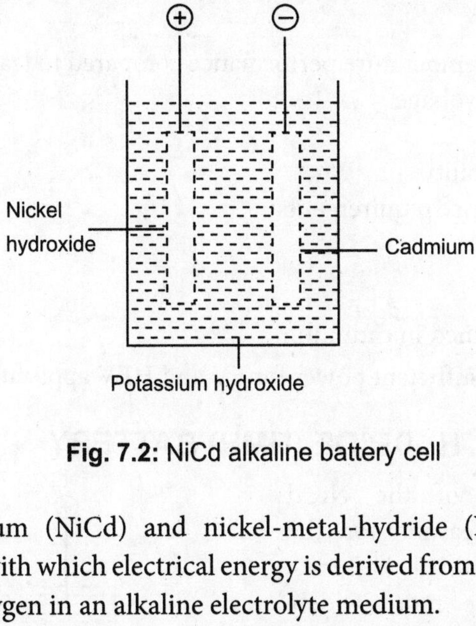

Fig. 7.2: NiCd alkaline battery cell

Nickel-cadmium (NiCd) and nickel-metal-hydride (NiMH) batteries are alkaline batteries with which electrical energy is derived from the chemical reaction of a metal with oxygen in an alkaline electrolyte medium.

Nickel-cadmium batteries are available for EVs applications, although they may not be advisable due to cadmium toxicity and nickel carcinogenity. They do not have the same life span as the nickel-metal hydride batteries.

The main components of the nickel-cadmium cell for vehicle use are as follows:

- Positive plate – Nickel oxide hydroxide (NiOOH)
- Negative plate – Cadmium (Cd)
- Electrolyte – Potassium hydroxide (KOH) and water (H_2O)

The process of charging involves the oxygen moving from the negative plate to the positive plate, and the reverse when discharging. When fully charged, the negative plate becomes pure cadmium and the positive plate becomes nickel oxide hydroxide. Fig. 7.2 shows a simplified representation of a NiCd battery cell.

A simplified chemical equation to represent this reaction is given below.

$$2NiOOH + Cd + 2H_2O + KOH \longleftrightarrow 2Ni(OH)_2 + CdO_2 + KOH$$

The $2H_2O$ is actually given off as hydrogen (H) and oxygen (O_2) as gassing takes place all the time during charge. The electrolyte does not change during the reaction. This means that a relative density reading will not indicate the state of charge. These batteries do not suffer from over-charging because once the cadmium oxide has changed to cadmium, no further reaction can take place.

The cell voltage of a fully charged cell is 1.4V but this falls rapidly to 1.3V as soon as discharge starts. The cell is discharged at a cell voltage of 1.1V. The specific energy of NiCd batteries is 30 to 50 Wh/kg, which is similar to that of lead-acid batteries.

Advantages

1. Superior low-temperature performance compared to lead-acid batteries
2. Flat discharge voltage
3. Long life
4. Excellent reliability
5. Low maintenance requirements

Disadvantages

1. High cost
2. Toxicity contained in cadmium
3. Developing insufficient power for EV and HEV applications

NICKEL-METAL HYDRIDE (NMH) BATTERY

The disadvantages of the NiCd batteries are the reasons for the development of NiMH batteries. NiMH batteries are more widely used by HEVs, but are also used successfully in some BEV cars. Nickel-metal hydride batteries have the advantages of high specific energy and long cycle life relative to lead-acid batteries (nearly double the energy density and two to four times the life). An important feature of this battery is that they can be fully charged with very little impact on battery life. They operate at ambient temperature and do not require maintenance.

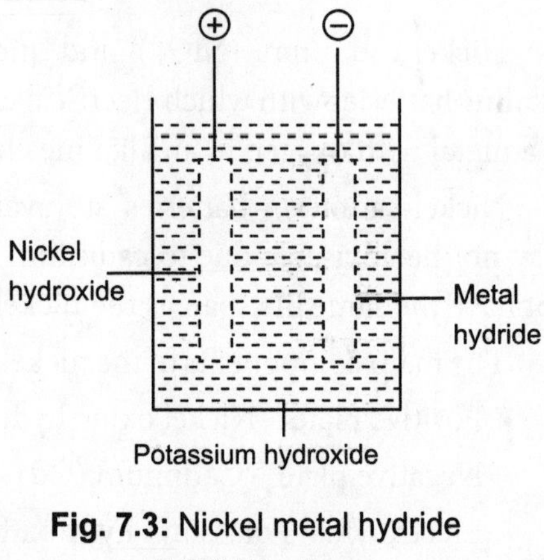

Fig. 7.3: Nickel metal hydride (NiMH) battery

The nickel-metal-hydride battery is a successor to the nickel-hydrogen battery and is already in use in production HEVs. In NiMH batteries, the positive electrode is a nickel hydroxide similar to that used in a NiCd battery, while the negative electrode is a metal hydride where hydrogen is stored. The concept of NiMH batteries is based on the fact that fine particles of certain metallic alloys, when exposed to hydrogen at certain pressures and temperatures absorb large quantities of the gas to form the metalhydride compounds. Furthermore, the metal hydrides are able to absorb and release hydrogen many times without deterioration. The two electrode chemical reactions in a NiMH battery are:

At the positive electrode,

$$NiOOH + H_2O + e^- \underset{\text{Charge}}{\overset{\text{Discharge}}{\rightleftharpoons}} Ni(OH)_2 + OH^-$$

At the negative electrode,

$$MH_x + OH^- \underset{\text{Charge}}{\overset{\text{Discharge}}{\rightleftharpoons}} MH_{x-1} + H_2O + e^-$$

"M" stands for metallic alloy, which takes up hydrogen at ambient temperature to form the metal hydride MH_X. The negative electrode consists of a compressed mass of fine metal particles. NiMH cells can last 40% longer than the same size NiCd cells and will have a life-span of up to 600 cycles. This makes them useful for high energy devices such as laptop computers, cellular phones, and camcorders.

Advantages

1. Charge up quickly
2. High cycle stability
3. 20% higher specific energy and power, and in volumetric terms 40% higher
4. Longer life cycle than Li-ion and lead-acid batteries
5. Safe and abuse tolerant.

Disadvantages

1. Relatively high cost
2. Higher self-discharge rate compared to NiCd
3. Poor charge acceptance capability at elevated temperatures
4. Low cell efficiency.

Generate significant heat at high temperatures

These deficiencies make NiMH less effective as a battery for electric cars whose batteries must be able to be recharged from outside the system, such as from the PLN network. That is why the car battery is the most widely applied by hybrid cars.

Table 7.3: NiMH battery parameters

Mass energy density	40-120 wh/kg
Volume energy density	140-400 wh/L
Powerdensity	300-1000 w/kg
Efficiency	65-180%
Self-discharge rate	~30% / month
Cycle durability	500-1000 cycles
Typical cost	₹ 23-46 / wh

LITHIUM-ION BATTERY

Lithium-ion (Li-ion) battery is now used primarily for electric vehicles, as they are much lighter which provides a more fuel efficient vehicle. These are very expensive batteries, and starting costs for cars are about ₹ 60,000. This battery may already be familiar to us because it is also used in many portable electronic equipment such as cell phones and laptops. The main difference is a matter of scale. Its physical capacity and size on electric cars is much greater – this is often referred to as a traction battery pack.

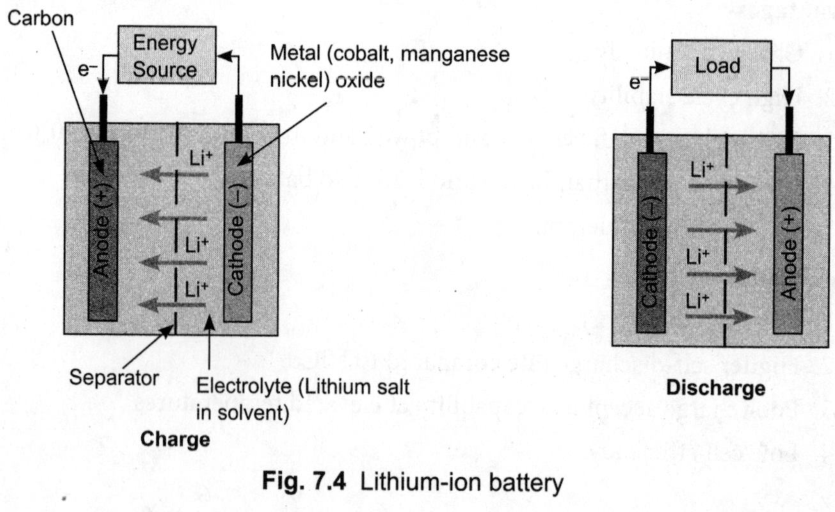

Fig. 7.4 Lithium-ion battery

Li-ion batteries have a very high power to weight ratio. This type of electric car battery has high energy efficiency. Performance at high temperatures is also good. The battery has a greater energy ratio per weight – a parameter that is very important for electric car batteries. The smaller the battery weight (same kWH capacity) means the car can travel further with a single charge.

This battery also has a low "self-discharge" level, so the battery is better than any other battery in maintaining its ability to hold its full charge.

In addition, most parts of Li-ion batteries can be recycled, making it the right choice for those interested in environmentally conscious electric cars. BEV cars and PHEVs use the most lithium batteries.

Charging reactions

Cathode reaction: $LiCoO_2 \rightarrow Li_{1-x}CoO_2 + xLi^+ + xe^-$

Anode reaction: $C + xLi^+ + xe^- \rightarrow CLi_x$

Battery as a whole: $LiCoO_2 + C \rightarrow Li_{1-x}CoO_2 + CLi_x$

Discharging reactions

Cathode reaction: $LiCoO_2 \rightarrow Li_{1-x}CoO_2 + xLi^+ + xe^-$

Anode reaction: $C + xLi^+ + xe^- \rightarrow CLi_x$

Battery as a whole: $LiCoO_2 + C \rightarrow Li_{1-x}CoO_2 + CLi_x$

Li-ion cells, in their most common form, consist of a graphite anode, a lithium metal oxide cathode and an electrolyte of a lithium salt and an organic solvent. Lithium is a good choice for an electrochemical cell due to its large standard electrode potential (3.04 V) resulting in a high operating voltage (which helps both power and energy) and the fact that it is the metal with the lowest density (which reduces weight). In an automotive application a Li-ion battery consists of tens to thousands of individual cells packaged together to provide the required voltage, power and energy.

Li-ion battery types

- Lithium Iron Phosphate ($LiFePO_4$) — LFP
- Lithium Nickel Cobalt Aluminum Oxide ($LiNiCoAlO_2$) — NCA
- Lithium Nickel Manganese Cobalt Oxide ($LiNiMnCoO_2$) — NMC
- Lithium Titanate (Li_2TiO_3) — LTO
- Lithium Manganese Oxide ($LiMn_2O_4$) — LMO
- Lithium Cobalt Oxide ($LiCoO_2$) — LCO

Advantages over conventional batteries

1. Higher specific energy
2. Higher specific power
3. High power to weight ratio. Up to 80% weight saving
4. Charge and discharge at high currents
5. Low self-discharge
6. Offer phenomenal starting power and massive deep cycle reserve power. They are capable of providing engine cranking pulses of 2250 amps for 5 seconds.
7. Longer life span with a minimum of 5 years' service life, up to 10 years depending on use.
8. No harmful emissions
9. Loss of voltage over discharge

Disadvantages

1. Heat
2. Higher initial cost

Table 7.4: Li-ion battery parameters

Mass energy density	100-180 wh/kg
Volume energy density	200-300 wh/L
Powerdensity	1000-5000 w/kg
Charge/Discharge Efficiency	95-99%
Mass energy density	100-180 wh/kg
Self-discharge rate	1-5% / month
Cycle durability	500-15000 cycles
Typical cost	$ 0.50-$2.50/wh
Self-discharge rate	1-5% / month

ZEBRA Batteries

ZEBRA batteries is actually a Zealite Battery Research Africa then became a Zero Emission Batteries Research Activity battery.

It is technically known as the sodium-nickle-chloride battery and some times as a sodium-metal-halid battery. ZEBRA batteries use plain salt and nickle as the raw material for their electrodes in combination with a ceramic electrolyte and a molton salt. This combination provides a battery system related specific energy of 120 Wh/kg and a specific power of 180 W/kg. With these data the battery is well designed for all types of electric and hybrid electric buses.

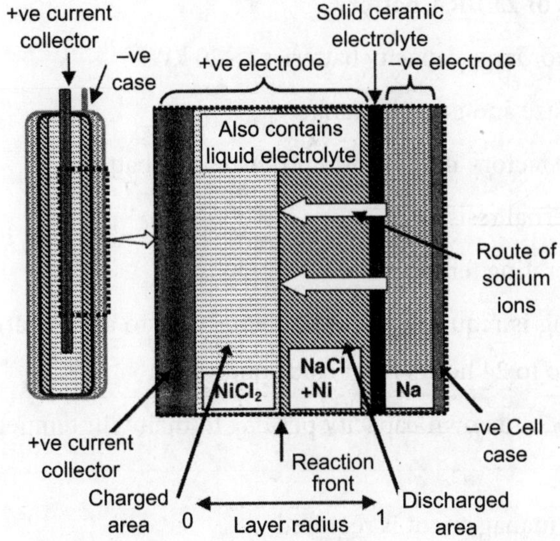

(a) Zebra cell (b) Enlarged internal portion

Fig. 7.5: ZEBRA batteries

This battery consists of a liquid Na negative electrode and $NiCl_2$ separated by β-alumina solid electrolyte with Na^+ conduction. Total cell reaction is as follows:

$$2Na + NiCl_2 \rightarrow 2NaCl + NiCl = 2.58V \text{ at } 300°C$$

Characteristics of ZEBRA batteries

1. High power cell so that it fits as an electric car battery
2. High temperature batteries operate at more than 270°C
3. The chemical Sodium Nickel Chloride (NaNiCl) provides a nominal operating cell voltage of 2.58 Volts

Advantages of ZEBRA battery

1. High energy density (5 times higher than Lead-acid batteries)
2. Large cells (up to 500Ah) allow
3. Life cycle> 1000 cycles
4. Short circuit tolerance
5. Safer than Sodium Sulphur cells
6. The typical cell failure is shorted but does not cause the battery to fully damage.
7. Low cost ingredients

Disadvantages of ZEBRA battery

1. Suitable for large capacity batteries (> 20 kWh)
2. Limited size and capacity range
3. Only one factory in the world produces this battery.
4. High internal resistance
5. High operating temperature.
6. Preheating is required to get the battery up to an operating temperature of 270°C (up to 24 hours from cold conditions)
7. Uses 14% of its own capacity per day to maintain temperature when not in use.
8. Thermal management is required

Table 7.5: Various type of batteries used in EVs

Company	Brand	Battery type
Maruti Suzuki	Ciaz	Li-ion
Mahindra	Scorpio Hybrid	Li-ion
TATA	Megapixel	Li-ion
Toyota	Prius (PHEV)	NiMH
	Camry Hybrid	NiMH
Honda	Civic Hybrid	NiMH
Hyundai	i10 Electric	Li-Polymer
BMW	i3 & i8	Li-ion

PERFORMANCE PARAMETERS OF A BATTERY

Below is a short description of performance parameters which are important in determining which battery should be used for a particular EV application.

Specific energy density

Specific energy of the batteries is their capacity for storing energy per kilogram of weight. This value is still only 1 percent of the specific energy of gasoline. However the amount of energy that a battery can hold depends on different factors like the temperature, humidity and the rate at which the battery is discharged. Battery cells today can reach nominal energy densities of 140 to 170 wh/kg, compared with 13000 wh/kg for gasoline. The specific energy of a battery determines the vehicle range.

NOTE:

Specific energy is same as energy density. But technically, energy density is a measure of energy stored per unit volume, while specific energy density is a measure of energy stored per unit mass.

Table 7.6 : Relative energy and power densities of different energy storage systems

Storage	Energy Density	Power Density
Battery	High	Low
Ultracapacitor	Low	High
Fuel cell	High	Low
Flywheel	Low	High

Specific power (or) Power density

Specific power is an important factor for determining acceleration. Specific power is the amount of power that batteries can deliver per kg of mass. Currently, batteries' performance in terms of specific power equals or exceeds that of internal combustion engines. Specific power is highest when the battery is fully charged. As the battery is discharged, the specific power decreases and acceleration also decreases. Specific power is usually measured at 80% depth of discharge.

Specific power is particularly important in hybrid vehicles, which discharge a small amount of energy quickly. In EVs, specific power is less important than specific energy.

Cycle life

Cycle life is the measure of the total number of times a battery can be discharged and charged during its life. When the battery can no longer hold a charge over 80%, its cycle life is considered to be finished. This is typically between 500 and 1200 cycles. Batteries for electric vehicles should last as long as the lifetime of the vehicle. Otherwise replacement of the car battery is necessary within the lifetime of the car. This will increase the price of driving a BEVs.

Shelf life

The battery shelf life is the time a battery can be stored inactive before its capacity falls to 80%. The reduction in capacity with time is caused by the depletion of the active materials by undesired reactions within the cell.

Efficiency

The efficiency of a battery is given by the energy losses that occur when charged and discharged. The amount of energy that is available to power the wheels represents the efficiency of the battery.

MEMORY EFFECT

Some types of batteries, such as nickel-cadmium, nickel-metal hydride and Lithium-ion, can develop a memory effect when only partially discharged before recharging. This "memory" reduces the capacity of subsequent charges and thus future battery life in a given device. The effect can also be caused by poorly-designed chargers.

The memory effect can be reduced by diligent battery use: fully discharging and recharging. One can recondition batteries with a memory effect by deep discharge and charge cycles. Some chargers have specific battery reconditioning modes as well.

The other terms used for memory effect are voltage depression of a battery, battery effect, lazy battery effect or battery memory.

ALTERNATIVE ENERGY STORAGE DEVICES

There have been various alternative energy storage devices including the flywheel and super capacitors. As a general rule both of these devices have high specific powers, which means that they can take in and give out energy very quickly. However, the amount of energy they can store is currently rather small. In other words, although they have a good power density, they have a poor energy density.

ULTRA CAPACITOR

Ultra capacitors, otherwise known as super capacitors or electrochemical capacitors, are different from batteries. Batteries store their energy chemically where an ultra capacitor stores it physically.

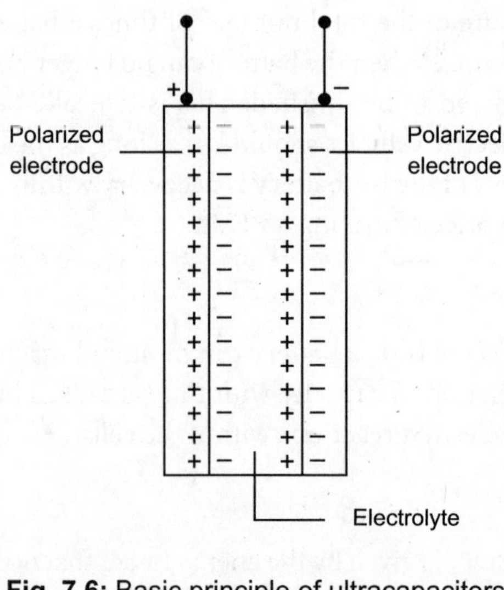

Fig. 7.6: Basic principle of ultracapacitors

A capacitor is a device for storing electrical energy in a dielectric placed between two conducting plates. Small volume capacitors are used frequently in numerous types of electric circuits. Their capacity is directly proportional to the area of the conducting plates. Thus if large-area capacitors used, they gain a high storage potential. If the capacity per unit weight is the same or greater than the secondary battery it becomes possible to use it as an EV battery. Alternatively, using a material whose surface has numerous small holes in it would reduce the size of the capacitor.

In an electric car, an ultra capacitor can provide the power needed for acceleration, while a battery provides range and recharges the ultra capacitor between surges. Ultra capacitors can be charged and discharged much faster than batteries and are very suitable for storing the energy from regenerative braking, for climbing hills or sudden acceleration.

In China and many other places around the world now, super capacitors are being used as main power source for buses, where they are charged en route at intervals in just about 30 seconds. Ultra capacitors use in buses, trams and trains is increasing.

Principle

The double-layer capacitor technology is the major approach to achieve the ultra capacitor concept. The basic principle of a double-layer capacitor is illustrated in Fig. 7.5. When a voltage is applied across the electrodes, a double layer is formed by the dipole orientation and alignment of electrolyte molecules over the entire surface of the electrodes. By adopting high-dielectric materials, short separation distances and large electrode surface areas, the capacitance can be greatly increased. At the present status of ultra capacitor technology, the corresponding electrode materials may be carbon/metal fibre composites, doped conducting polymer films on carbon cloth or mixed metal oxide coatings on metal foil, while the electrolyte materials may be aqueous/organic solution or solid polymer.

Characteristics of ultracapacitors

Capacitors have a number of great properties. They store power as electrical charge rather than chemical energy. This typically allows near instant charge times and very high peak output currents. They can survive hundreds of thousands of charge-discharge cycles, rather than the hundreds of cycles for full-cycled batteries. Ultracapacitors have little or no internal resistance (down to 0 to 12 mΩ), allowing them to work at close to 100% efficiency.

A battery's voltage stays nearly constant as it discharges at a constant current. Thus the power output is nearly constant. A capacitor's voltage drops linearly over time at a constant current. Thus, power output drops linearly. In order to use the capacitor as a battery replacement, you need a voltage regulation circuit that can step up voltage as it drops, which means you need a linear increase in current output to deliver a constant power output.

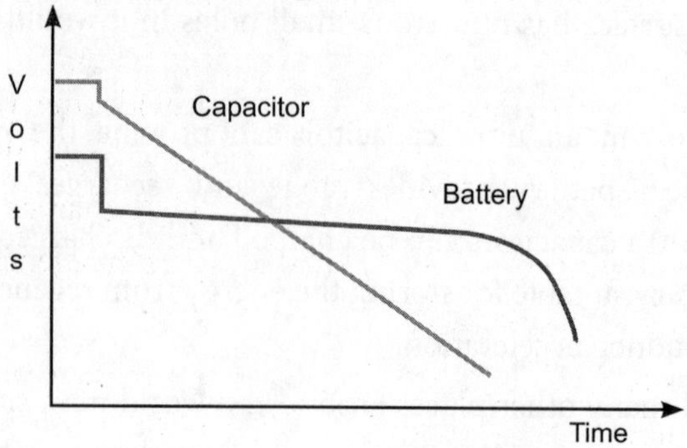

Fig. 7.7: Dischange cycle

The other problem is that modern ultracapacitors have much lower specific energy than batteries. The ultracapacitor has much higher specific power, but much lower specific energy compared to the chemical batteries. Its specific energy is in the range of a few watt-hours per kilogram. However, its specific power can reach up to 5 kW/kg, much higher than any type of battery. Due to their low specific energy density and the dependence of voltage on the state-of-charge, it is difficult to use ultracapacitors alone as an energy storage for EVs and HEVs.

Supercapacitors do not go anywhere near the energy density of batteries today at current status of development. So they cannot run car over long distances like batteries. However they are used in modern cars, both EVs and hybrid vehicles in combination with batteries, to extend life of batteries and take over number of functions of batteries, and get better performance in the process. Ultracapacitor technology is ideally suited to regenerative braking and start-stop systems. Start-stop applications enable an engine to shut down when it comes to a stop at a red light, or when sitting in traffic. Ultracapacitors then provide a short burst of energy that restarts the motor.

Ultracapacitors are good partners for Li-ion batteries and other high-energy-density storage technologies. The two can be connected in parallel to create combined power supply units. Due to load leveling, ultracapacitors can significantly expand battery life and improve safety.

The power density of ultracapacitors is up to 60 times greater than batteries. This high power density means it's possible to recharge large banks of ultracapacitors in just three or four seconds. This means they are ideally suited for applications that require high bursts of power.

Advantages

1. Can store 10 to 100 times more energy per unit volume or unit mass than standard electrolytic capacitors
2. Can be charged and discharged more quickly (almost instantly) than batteries
3. Tolerate many more charge/discharge cycles than rechargeable batteries
4. Able to provide large surges of power in short periods of time without overheating.
5. Deliver many times more power for weight than Li-ion batteries.
6. They have efficiencies of up to 98%.
7. Unlimited cycle life (over 1 million cycles)
8. Tolerant of high temperatures.
9. One of the cheapest technologies available for power discharges below 15 secs.

Disadvantages

1. Only about 1/10 the energy density of batteries (and thus are physically larger for a given amount of energy)
2. Low maximum voltage
3. Extremely high capital cost

FLYWHEEL

The flywheel is an energy storage device, similar to a battery, but instead of storing the energy chemically, it is stored in kinetic form in a rotating disc. Typically, the rotor is accelerated by an electric motor (charging process) and decelerated when the motor is switched to generative operation (discharging).

This flywheel energy system composed of composite rotors spinning at thousands of rpm on frictionless magnetic bearings, which can drive a generator to provide power for EVs. Energy stored in flywheels increases quadratically with rotational speed of the rotors. As energy is used up, the rotor slows. American Flywheel Systems developed a first generation EV flywheel. This company claimed that the flywheel is of the same size as the 6-volt battery, but weighs much less, stores 3 times the energy and lasts ten times longer. Gyroscopic effect is avoided by having two adjoining wheels counter rotating at identical speeds on a stationary shaft. Friction is reduced to negligible levels by suspending the wheels in vacuum.

The company speculates that the range would be extended to 300 miles on a single charge in relation to that of lead-acid battery. The life of the flywheel would, theoretically be very long and no replacement would be needed relative to the chemical battery systems.

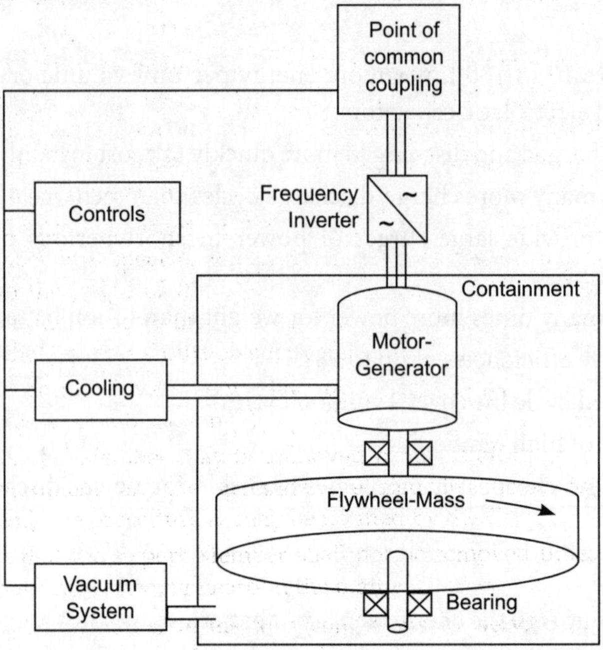

Fig. 7.8: Flywheel

The importance of energy storage with flywheel is to reduce the loss of mechanical energy, namely the loss of kinetic energy that consists of air friction resistance and rotary resistance. According to different means for the reduction of energy loss, Flywheel energy storage system (FESS) can be divided into low-speed flywheel system and high-speed flywheel system. The first reduces air friction by increasing the mass of flywheel while the second is to reduce the air pressure of operating environment of flywheel. The high-speed flywheel system benefits from the use of high strength compound material (carbonic fibre). It has characteristics of small mass, low volume and high speed. Thus it is fit for vehicle using.

The high-speed flywheel system consists mainly of a flywheel, a motor and a generator. It is connected with exterior electrical systems through input or output electronic equipments and the power transported from exterior systems is converted from electric energy into mechanical energy by raising rotary speed of flywheel. When it is needed to output power, mechanical energy is converted back into electric energy through generator and meantime the rotary speed of flywheel is reduced. The motor and generator are usually integrated together and magnetic suspension bearings are adopted by flywheel system, through the support of which the flywheel is fixed in a vacuum container.

Advantages

There are factors that make the flywheel attractive for use as energy storage:

1. High power density
2. Long cycle life
3. No degradation over time
4. Easily estimated state-of-charge
5. Highest energy storage density
6. Shortest charging time
7. Easiest maintenance
8. No pollution

Disadvantages

1. Excessive high cost. Its cost is about 1.5 times that of ultra-capacitor and is about 6 ~ 7 times that of chemical battery.

Table 7.7: Comparison between Battery, Ultracapacitor and Flywheel

	Battery	Ultracapacitor	Flywheel
Storage mechanism	Chemical	Electric	Mechanical
Life	3-5 Years	Years	> 20 Years
Temperature range	Limited	Limited	Less limited
Relative mass (Equivalent energy)	Large	Middle	Small
Time to hold a charge	Months	Days	Hours

REVIEW QUESTIONS

1. Are Electric vehicles (EVs) better for the environment than Internal Combustion Engine (ICE) vehicles?
2. What is the impact of battery manufacturing and production on the environment?
3. What materials is an average EV Lithium-Ion Battery composed of?
4. What is the average lifetime of a lithium-ion EV battery?
5. Can lithium and other materials contained in the EV batteries be recycled?
6. Do I need to fully charge my EV battery every day?
7. How is range affected by extreme ambient temperatures?

8. How do we make batteries less expensive?
9. How can we make batteries that store more energy?
10. How can we make batteries safer?
11. Are batteries enough for a renewable grid?
12. Which battery is best for electric vehicle?
13. What is a valid issue with electric vehicle batteries?
14. Do batteries have electrical energy?
15. How long will a lithium battery last if not charged?
16. What's the Lifespan of an Electric Car Battery?

8 ELECTRIC MOTOR

UNIT OUTCOMES

Upon successful completion of this module, the student will be able to:

1. Study the requirements of EVs motor.
2. Identify the major types of electric motors for EVs
3. Get exposed to parameters that affect the performance of a motor.

The motor is to an EV which engine is to the IC engine. Electric motors convert electrical energy into mechanical energy. Two types of electric motors are used in electric vehicles to provide power to the wheels: the direct current (DC) motor and the alternating current (AC) motor.

DC motors are larger and more complicated than AC motors, and it is difficult to make them highly efficient. On the benefit side, however, is that the DC motor's controller can be easily made. As a result, most of the EVs use DC motors. The features of the AC motor are just the opposite. Advances of semiconductor field can be used to make the DC-AC inverter for the AC motor's controller highly efficient and small in size. The combination of motor and controller is making the AC motor gradually superior in terms of the efficiency, price and size.

However, with the advent of better and less expensive electronics, a large number of today's electric vehicles are using AC motor/controller systems because of their improved motor efficiency and lighter weight.

Because the controller provides electrical power from the traction battery, the electric traction motors will work turning the transmission and wheels. Some hybrid electric cars use a type of generator-motor that performs the functions of propulsion and regeneration. In general, the type of electric motor used is the BLDC (brushless DC) motor.

Requirements of EV Motor

The electric motors used for automotive applications should have characteristics like high starting torque, high power density and efficiency

The other requirements of the EV motors are summarized as follows:

1. High torque at low speeds and climbing as well as high speed at low torques for cruising
2. Very wide speed range including constant-torque and constant-power regions
3. Fast torque response
4. High efficiency for regenerative braking
5. High reliability and robustness for various vehicle operating conditions
6. Reasonable cost.

Types of Electric Motors

Today's automotive use three difference types of electric motors in EVs: the brushed DC motor, BLDC motor and AC induction motor.

BRUSHED DC MOTOR

The simplest motor that can be used in automotive applications is the brushed DC motor. This motor is used in all sorts of domestic electric appliances like hairdryers and fans. In Fig. 8.1 a two-pole brushed DC motor is shown with one coil. The

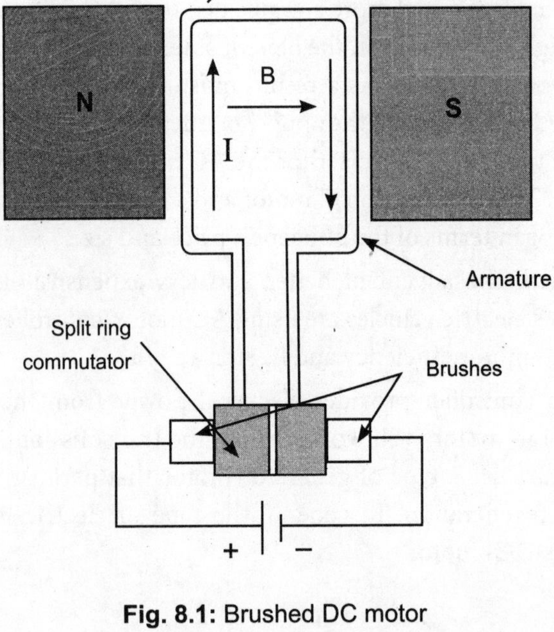

Fig. 8.1: Brushed DC motor

motor consists of a stator with two permanent magnets and brushes and a rotor (coil) with commutator and windings. The force on the left side is upwards where the force on the right side is downwards, causing the coil to turn clockwise. When the wires of the coil with the commutator are clear of the magnets momentum carries the rotor halfway around until it connect with the brushes again. The commutator is constantly changing the direction of the current to assure that the forces are pushing the coil clockwise.

A real DC motor however is using a rotor with multiple coils and a stator with more than one pair of magnets but the principle remains the same. There are three basic brushed DC motors; a series, parallel and separately excited brushed DC motor as shown in Fig. 8.2. DC series motors was a widely used motor back in the 1990s. This motor in capable of producing high initial torque. The easy speed control and sudden load increase bearing capacity make these motors a good choice. For use in electric vehicles the one that can be used is the separately exited motor. The required torque can be controlled at any angular speed giving the motor great flexibility.

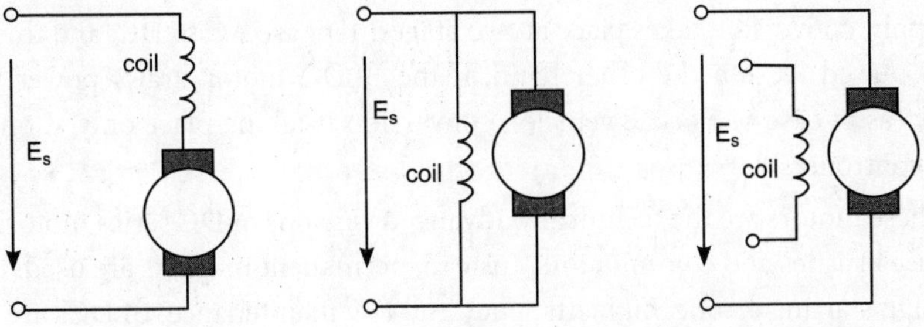

Fig. 8.2: Basic brushed DC motors

Due to the brushes making physical contact with the commutator, sparking is a common issue with brushed motors. They are causing friction, limit the speed range and need regular maintenance. These motors are still in use by the indian railways.

BRUSHLESS DC MOTOR

A BLDC motor (brushless DC motor) should always be viewed as a combination of controller and motor (it can't run without a controller) and the controller takes DC input. The controller is a static unit which converts DC into pulsed AC whereas motor is an electromagnetic rotating machine which runs on pulsed AC.A BLDC motor is also called DC synchronous motor or electronically commutated DC motor.

The input to the controller is a DC voltage. Controller converts DC voltage into 2-phase or 3-phase AC, which is fed to motor electromagnets. Note that the AC produced by controller is not pure AC (sinusoidal wave) but of rectangular or pulsed waveform. When the stator electromagnets are energised by pulsed AC from controller, there is a continuous change in the polarity of stator electromagnets in a sequential manner which, in effect, causes rotation of stator magnetic field. The rotor permanent magnets follow the stator rotating field due to magnetic pull, hence the rotation. The motor, thus, works like a synchronous motor. As the primary source of power for this motor is DC (through controller), it is sometimes called DC synchronous motor.

In a BLDC motor, the input motor current is reversed at the appropriate moment depending upon the rotor position (as signalled by hall effect sensor). This is something like the action a mechanical commutator in a conventional DC motor. Hence the BLDC motor is also, sometimes, called electronically commutated DC motor.

It is interesting to note that if BLDC motor draws power from home 1-phase AC supply, conversion takes place at two stages: 1-phase AC to DC, and then from DC to pulsed AC.On the other hand, if the BLDC motor draws power from a battery (as in case of electric vehicle), conversion is taking place only at one stage in the controller.

These motors are the technically advanced versions of DC series motors. They don't use brushes and commutators. Instead, permanent magnets are used. BLDCs have high starting torque, high efficiency and low maintenance. BLDCs are widely used these days either as the hub motor or belt-driven.

Operation

The motor has a three-phase stator with a number of coils and a rotor with surface mounted permanent magnets. The stator and the rotor are reversed compared to the brushed DC motor where the permanent magnets are mounted on the stator.

The way a BLDC motor works is that the poles on the stator are alternating, in such a way that the rotor is turning clockwise. The pole on the stator pulls the pole on the rotor clockwise and when the poles are in line with each other the current is switched off. Momentum then carries the rotor further and the current is reversed, changing the magnetic field and the poles in the stator. To make sure the motor keeps on turning sensors are needed to determine the position of the rotor. This is often done using Hall Effect sensors.

BLDC motors are very efficient. Torque is high under low speeds and goes down as the speed goes up. A drawback of this type of motor is the price compared to the other possible EV motors. A BLDC motor needs a strong permanent magnet that can influence the total price of the motor.

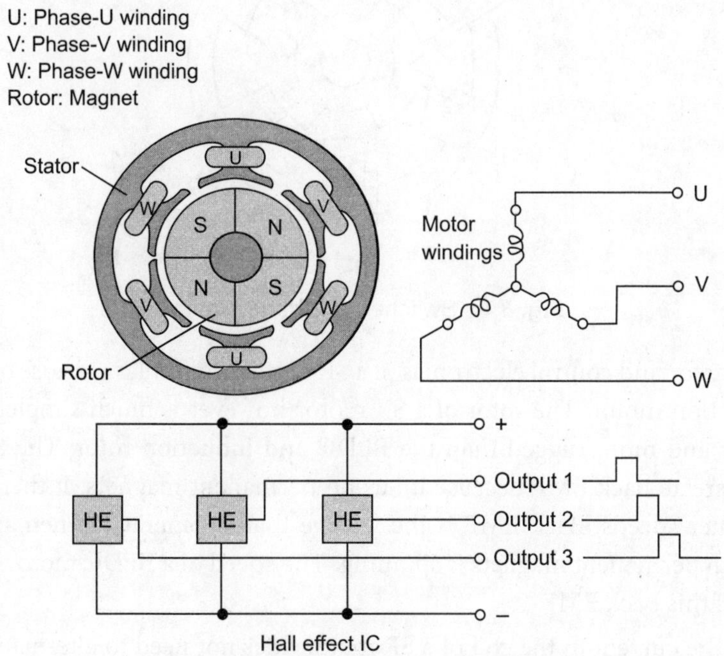

Fig. 8.3: Brushless DC motor

PERMANENT MAGNET SYNCHRONOUS MOTOR (PMSM)

It is very similar in construction to the BLDCs. But the major difference is in the back emf. PMSM has a sinusoidal back emf whereas BLDC has trapezoidal one. They have a high power rating and can be used in high-performance applications such as sports cars, buses etc. For e.g. Nissan Leaf and Toyota Prius use a PMSM for propulsion.

SWITCHED RELUCTANCE MOTOR

The switched reluctance (SR) motor is a simple motor with an iron rotor and stator. The stator is magnetised and attracts the rotor. When the rotor is aligned with the stator (magnetic field is symmetrical) the current is switched off and momentum carries the rotor further and the current is switched on again.

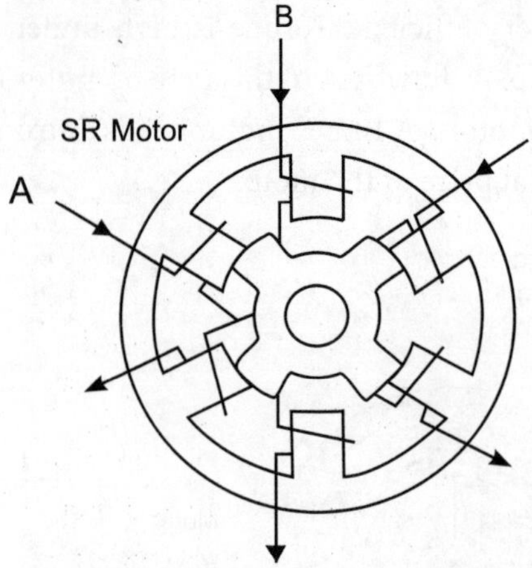

Fig. 8.4: Switched reluctance motor

The stator and control electronics of a SR motor are similar to those of a BLDC and induction motor. The rotor of a SR motor however is much simpler, making it cheaper and more rugged than the BLDC and induction rotor. The SR motor does not create back EMF because it has no permanent magnets. It therefore can reach higher speeds. Back EMF is the voltage that is generated when an electric motor with permanent magnets is spinning. The speed of a BLDC motor is limited because of this back EMF.

Also the current in the coil of a SR motor does not need to alternate. It needs an advanced control systems and sensors to adjust the speed and make sure the current is switched on and off on time. Another drawback of the motor is that it is known to be a bit noisy. SR motors are not used in commercial EVs and HEVs yet, but because of the good properties and possible low costs of the motor they will become more widespread in the future.

AC INDUCTION MOTOR

The technology of the induction motor is very mature and is used in all sorts of appliances like washing machines, pumps and industrial machines. Therefore it is a popular choice and most used in EVs and HEVs of today. Unlike the DC motors, induction motors do not have a high starting torque. It is cheap as compared to the other motors. It still has very high efficiency and can withstand rugged environmental conditions. Tesla model S use this type of motors. Even Tata and TVS are planning to use induction motors in their electric vehicles. Indian Railways have also started using induction motors over DC motors.

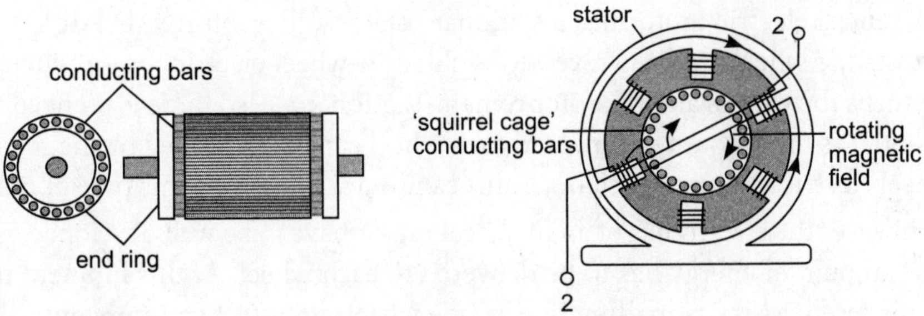

Fig. 8.5: AC induction motor

Instead of using a permanent magnet in the rotor (as in the BLDC motor), it is also possible to induce a current in the rotor to create a temporary magnet. This is done in an AC induction motor. The rotor type that is most common in an induction motor is the 'squirrel cage'. The rotor consists of a stack of steel laminations with evenly spaced conductor bars around the shaft. The conductor bars are forming a kind of cage. The conductor bars are electronically linked with end rings.

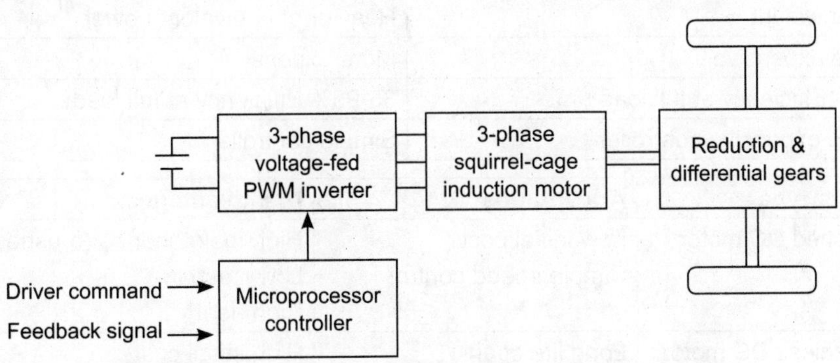

Fig. 8.6: Basic EV induction motor drive configuration

The rotor of an induction motor consists of a number of coils with the windings displaced by 120°. When a 3-phase AC is supplied to the rotor a current is induced in the conductor bars of the rotor. It will turn clockwise 'chasing' the magnetic field that is going anti-clockwise. The angular speed of the rotor is lower than the magnetic field. This so called 'slip' velocity is the relative velocity between the rotor speed and magnetic field.

IN-WHEEL MOTOR VERSUS CENTRAL MOTOR

The BEVs that are on the market (for example the Tesla Roadster and Think City) are equipped with a central electric AC induction motor. The central electric motor is cheaper to produce and is also more developed than the in-wheel electric motor.

A central electric motor has a stationary stator and a rotor with a differential that turns the wheels. This is reversed with an in-wheel electric motor where the stator turns the wheels and the rotor remains stationary. Also there is no need for a differential as the amount of power to each wheel can be controlled by the separate in-wheel electric motors. Efficiency gains can be achieved with this type of motor.

However the electronics of an in-wheel motor have to be well developed as the precise amount of energy has to be delivered to each wheel. At this moment there are some safety issues as malfunction of one wheel can result in an uncontrollable vehicle.

ELECTRIC MOTOR COMPARISON

Different type of electric motors used in EVs & HEVs are compared on the basis of certain parameters which should be considered for selecting a particular motor type for electric vehicles applications.

AC motor	DC motor
Single-speed transmission	Multi-speed transmission
Light weight	Heavier at equivalent power
Less expensive	More expensive
95% Efficiency at full load	85-95% Efficiency at full load
More expensive controller	Simple controller

Motor type	Advantages	Disadvantages
Brushed DC motor	Low initial cost Simple speed control	High maintenance (brushes) Low lifespan High heat
Brushless DC motor	Long life span Least rotor heat generated Low maintenance High peak efficiency High efficiency at lower load conditions Reliable	High initial cost Requires a controller Poor high speed capability Non-adjustable magnetic field
Switched reluctance motor	Low initial cost High average efficiency Highly reliable and robust Very simple control	High acoustic noise Requires large filter capacitor Failure of one leg phase does not interfere operation of remaining leg phases

Motor type	Advantages	Disadvantages
Induction motor	Low initial cost High power High average efficiency Light weight Small volume Mature technology	Rotation slips from frequency Accumulation of rotor heat

REVIEW QUESTIONS

1. How do I choose a motor for my electric car?
2. What features should an EV motor have?
3. What challenges do electric cars face?
4. Which motor is most commonly used in electric vehicles?
5. How does an electric motor differ from an internal combustion engine?
6. How does an electric motor behave differently from a combustion engine?
7. How is the power of an electric car calculated? And how is consumption measured?
8. How about the servicing and life of electric motors?
9. Which wheels does the electric motor provide drive to?
10. Do all electric cars have the same type of motor?
11. Is there a difference between the electric motors in plug-in hybrids and in pure electric cars?

9 CONTROL SYSTEMS

UNIT OUTCOMES

Upon successful completion of this module, the student will be able to:

1. Study the importance of motor controllers in EVs.
2. Identify the major types of controllers used for EVs

The most important system in an EV is the control system. The control system is responsible for governing the operation of the electric vehicle. The control system receives inputs from the operator, feedback signals from the motor controller, motor and also from other systems within the EV. The speed at which the control system must receive data from other systems, process the data in an algorithm and output a response to the given conditions must be accomplished in milli-seconds. This requires the control system to have a microprocessor to accomplish its tasks. Though no two control systems are identical, most of the feedback signals are similar. The table below lists common components of a control system and the feedback signals that are sent to the microprocessor.

Component	Feedback signal
Electric Motor(s)	Winding temperature Rotor speed (RPM)
Battery	Voltage Output current Temperature
Motor Controller	Current (and direction of current) Voltage Temperature Leakage current
Accelerator Pedal	Voltage as a function of pedal position
Shift Selector	Forward/Reverse Range selection

The control system must continuously monitor the feedback signals listed above. For instance, if the temperature of the windings in the motor gets too hot, the magnetic properties of that motor can be permanently altered or the windings may melt. By feeding a signal back to the microprocessor, the control system can limit the output of the motor if it senses a temperature rise. The same limiting or shutdown of any system can take place if an undesirable condition is or has occurred. Other feedback signals give information to the microprocessor to control the speed of the vehicle. The accelerator pedal functions in much the same way as conventional vehicles. As the pedal is depressed, an increasing signal voltage (not traction battery voltage) is sent to the microprocessor which instructs the motor controller to increase the amount of current in the motor windings, causing the motor to spin faster. As the signal voltage from the accelerator pedal is decreased, the motor spins slower.

In some advanced control systems, it is possible to limit the amount of current that flows to the motor, based on a switch selection. This allows the operator to adjust to a driving style that fits a particular situation. For instance, if a driver needs a certain range (in kms) from a single charge, the range selection can be set so that the microprocessor will limit the amount of output current from the motor controllers to a preset limit. If the preset limit is 100 amps, the microprocessor will not allow any current above this limit to flow to the motors. In this mode, acceleration ability is sacrificed for range. If the driver is in an area where the vehicle must climb steep grades, the range selector can be set so that the maximum current capability of the motor controller and motor can be used. The range selection feature is a valuable feature that adds to the efficiency of the motor controller. The ultimate goal of a control system is to maximise the energy stored within the traction battery and to prevent unsafe conditions from occurring within the electric vehicle.

MOTOR CONTROLLERS

The controller transforms the battery's direct current into alternating current for the AC motors or simply regulates current flow for DC motors. The controller will also reverse the motor rotation (so the vehicle can go in reverse), and convert the motor to a generator (so that the kinetic energy of motion can be used to recharge the battery when the brake is applied).

Variable-resistor-type controller

In the early electric vehicles with DC motors, a simple variable-resistor-type controller controlled the acceleration and speed of the vehicle. This regulates the flow of energy from the power pack to the motor in direct relation to pressure applied on the accelerator. With this type of controller, full current and power is drawn from the battery all of the time. At slow speeds, when full power is not needed, a high resistance is used to reduce the current to the motor. With this type of system, a large percentage of the energy from the battery is wasted as an energy loss in the resistor. The only time that all of the available power is used is at high speeds.

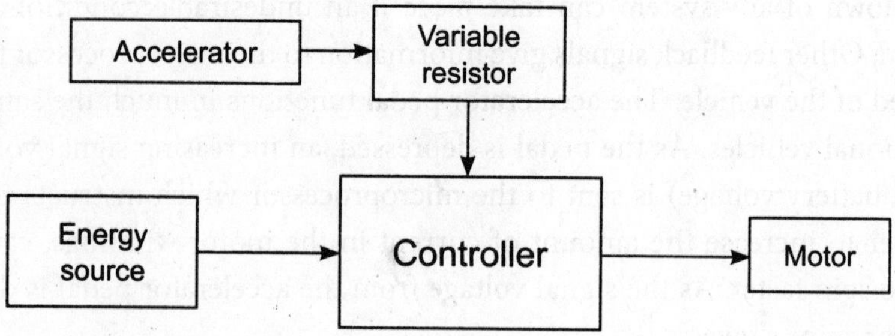

Fig. 9.1: Variable-resistor-type controller

Pulse-width Modulation

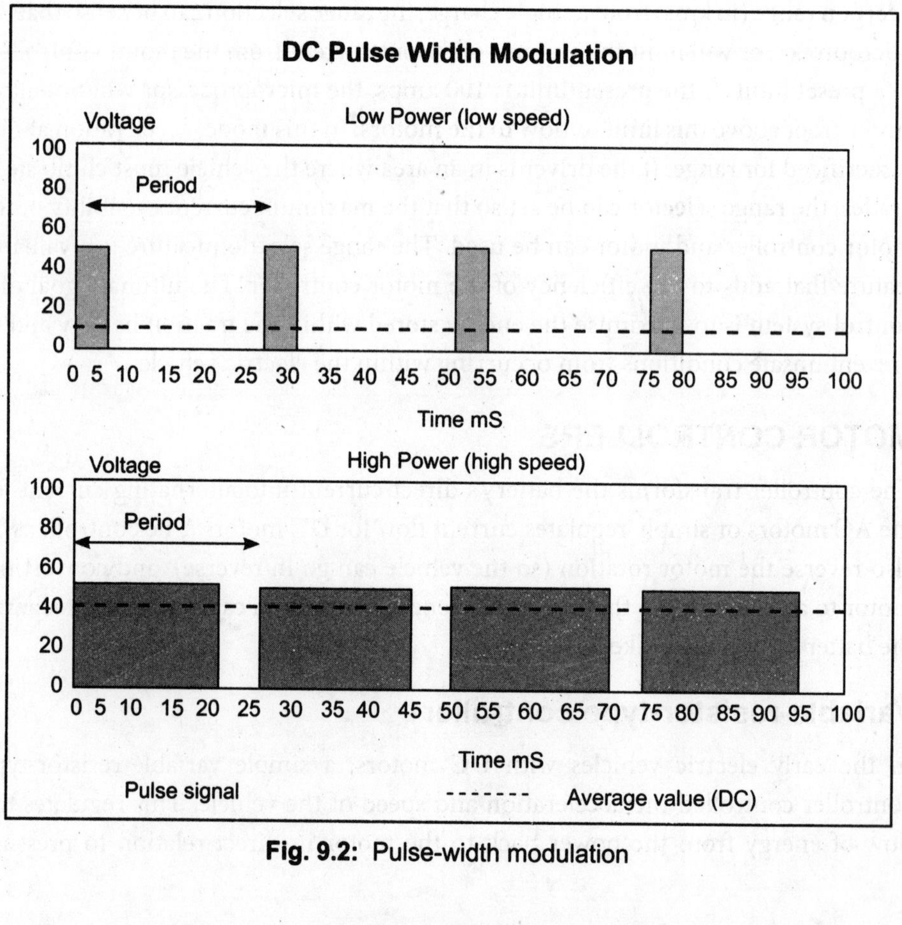

Fig. 9.2: Pulse-width modulation

Modern controllers adjust speed and acceleration by an electronic process called pulse width modulation. Switching devices such as silicone-controlled rectifiers rapidly interrupt (turn on and turn off) the electricity flow to the motor. High power (high speed and/or acceleration) is achieved when the intervals (when the current is turned off) are short. Low power (low speed and/or acceleration) occurs when the intervals are longer.

REVIEW QUESTIONS

1. What is the importance of motor controllers in EVs and HEVs?
2. List the components of a control system in EVs.
3. How do you classify the motor controllers used in EVs?

10 CONFIGURATIONS OF ELECTRIC VEHICLES

UNIT OUTCOMES

Upon successful completion of this module, the student will be able to:

1. Study the different configurations of EVs with reference to drive arrangement.

EVs can have different configurations with reference to drive arrangement as shown in Figs. 10.1 to 10.8.

With Clutch (Variable gearing transmission)

It has a gearbox and clutch that allows high torque at low speeds and low torque at high speeds. There is a differential as well that allows the wheels to rotate at different speeds. It is also classified as single-speed transmission. It has a single-speed fixed gearing. Based on fixed-gearing transmission, the motor should be so designed that it can provide both high instantaneous torque (3 to 5 times the rated value) in the constant-torque region and high operating speed (3 to 5 times the base speed) in the constant-power region. Actually, almost all the modern EVs adopt fixed-gearing transmission.

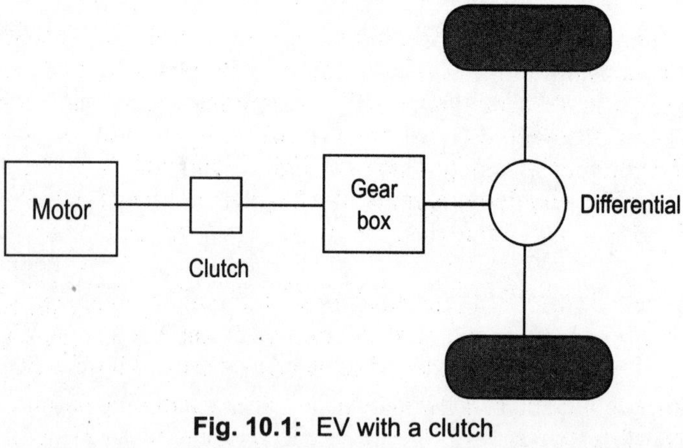

Fig. 10.1: EV with a clutch

Without clutch (Fixed gearing transmission)

Fig. 10.2 shows a configuration with the clutch omitted. It has a fixed gear in place of the gearbox which removes the chance of getting the desired torque-speed characteristics. It is also classified as multiple-speed transmission. It uses multiple-speed variable gearing together with the gearbox and clutch. The variable gearing transmission provides the advantage of using conventional motors to achieve high starting torque at low gear and high cruising speed at high gear. However, there are many drawbacks on the use of variable gearing such as the heavy weight, bulky size, high cost, less reliable and more complex.

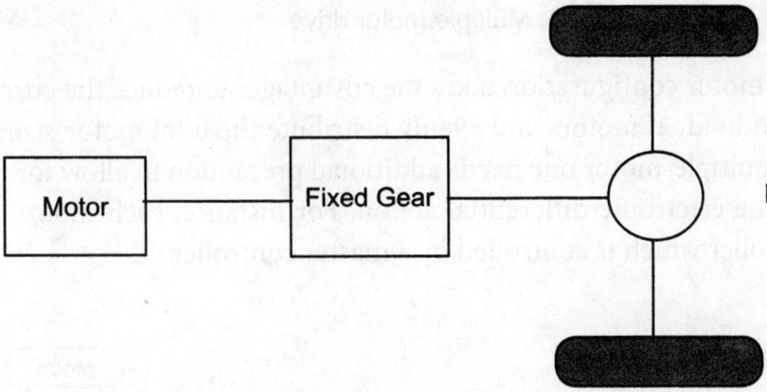

Fig. 10.2: EV without a clutch

Single motor

The configuration of Fig. 10.3 has the motor, gear and differential as a single unit that drives both the wheels. The Nissan Leaf, as well as the Chevrolet Spark, uses an electric motor mounted at the front to drive the front axle.

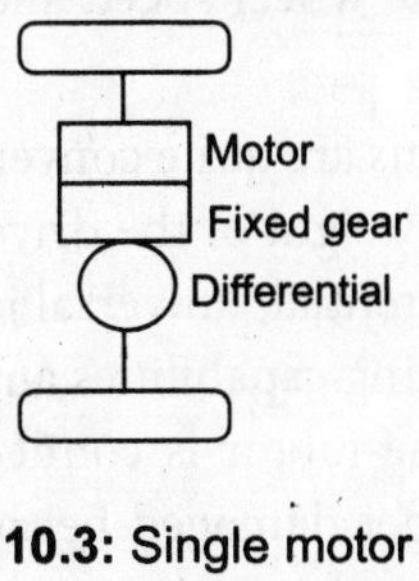

Fig. 10.3: Single motor drive

The single-motor configuration has the merit of using only one motor which can minimise the corresponding size, weight and cost.

Multiple motor

In Figs. 10.4 configurations to obtain differential action by using two motors for the two wheels are shown. A planetary gear system is employed here because advantages like high speed reduction ratio and inline arrangement of input and output shafts.

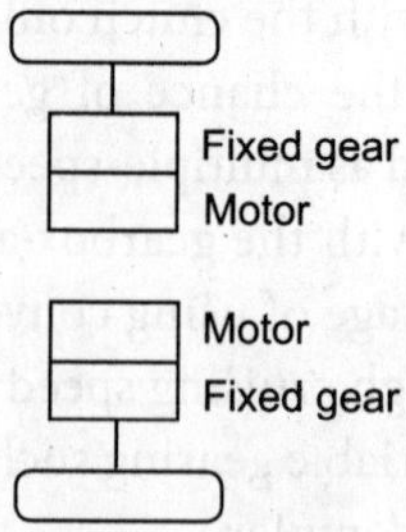

Fig. 10.4: Multiple motor drive

The multiple-motor configuration takes the advantages to reduce the current/ power ratings of individual motors and evenly distribute the total motor size and weight. Also, the multiple-motor one needs additional precaution to allow for fault tolerance during the electronic differential action. For instance, each motor may have its own controller which is controlled by a master controller.

In-wheel Drive

Mechanical interaction can be further reduced by placing the motors inside the wheels to produce an 'in-wheel drive'.

Mechanical gear system is totally removed in this configuration by mounting a low-speed motor with an outer rotor configuration on the wheel rim. Controlling the motor speed thus controls the wheel speed and the vehicle speed.

Fig. 10.5: In wheel drive

In-wheel motor configurations are quite convenient in the sense that they reduce the weight of the drive train by removing the central motor, related transmission, differential, universal joints and drive shaft. They also provide more control, better turning capabilities and more space for batteries, fuel cells or cargo, but in this case the motor is connected to the power and control systems through wires that can get damaged because of the harsh environment, vibration and acceleration, thus causing serious trouble.

In-wheel wire-less type

In this type, the wires are replaced by two coils which are able to transfer power in-between them. Because of vibrations caused by road conditions, the motor and the vehicle can be misaligned and can cause variation in the secondary side voltage. In conditions like this, magnetic resonance coupling is preferred for wireless power transfer as it can overcome the problems associated with such misalignments. Wireless power transfer (WPT) employing magnetic resonance coupling in a series-parallel arrangement can provide a transmitting efficiency of 90% in both directions at 2 kW. Therefore, wireless in-wheel motor configuration is compliant with regenerative braking as well.

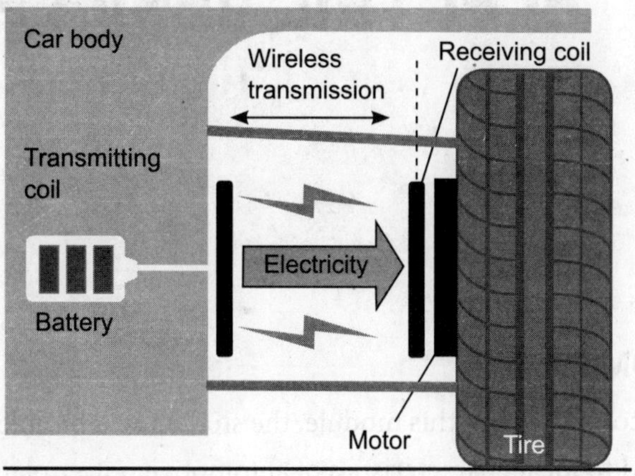

Fig. 10.6: In wheel wireless drive

REVIEW QUESTIONS

1. Classify the configurations of EVs with reference to drive arrangement.
2. List out the merits of single-motor configuration.
3. Give the importance of in-wheel drive configuration.

11 PERFORMANCE OF ELECTRIC VEHICLES

UNIT OUTCOMES

Upon successful completion of this module, the student will be able to:

1. Get exposed to ideal characteristics of automotive power plants.
2. Study the characteristics of electric motors for EVs and HEVs application.

Ideal Characteristics of Power Plants

For automotive applications, the ideal performance characteristic of a power plant is the constant power output over the full speed range. Consequently, the torque varies with speed hyperbolically as shown in Fig. 11.1

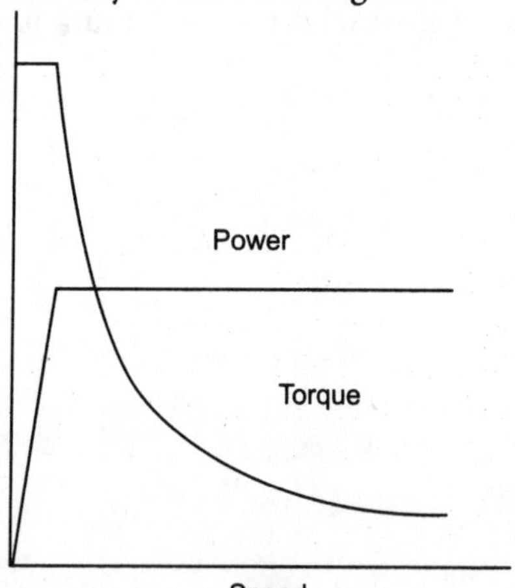

Fig. 11.1: Ideal performance characteristics for an automotive power plant

At low speeds, the torque is constrained to be constant so as not to be greater than the maximum limit set by the adhesion between the tyre–ground contact area.

The constant power characteristic will provide the vehicle with a high tractive effort at low speeds, where demands for acceleration, drawbar pull, or grade climbing capability are high.

Characteristics of a gasoline engine in full throttle

- The internal combustion engines usually have torque-speed characteristics far from the ideal performance characteristics of a power plant for automobiles.
- It starts operating smoothly at idle speed.
- Since the rate of doing work increases with piston speed, the engine's power will tend to rise with crankshaft speed of rotation. After about two thirds of the engine's speed range, the engine power output will decline. The slowing down and even decline in power at the upper speed range is mainly due to the very short time available for exhausting and for inducting fresh charge into the cylinders at very high speeds, with a resulting reduction in the cylinders' mean effective pressures. Therefore, the maximum permissible speed of the engine is usually set just a little above the speed of the maximum power output.

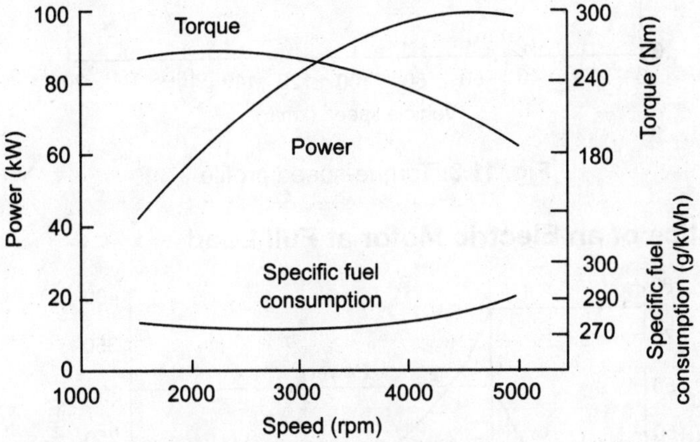

Fig. 11.2: Characteristics of a gasoline engine in full throttle

- The torque that an engine can develop changes with engine speed. An engine can develop more torque at intermediate speeds than at high speeds. This is because there is more time for air-fuel mixture to enter the cylinders.
- Volumetric efficiency is high. There will be a greater amount of air-fuel mixture to burn during the power stroke and higher combustion pressures will develop. This means, in turn, that greater torque will be applied to the crankshaft.

- The specific fuel consumption is lowest at the mixture ratio nearer to chemically correct mixture. If the mixture is richer or leaner than this, fuel consumption will be higher. A 4-stroke engine consumes least fuel in the medium engine speed. The specific fuel consumption rises at low speeds because of incomplete fuel-air mixing, but also at high engine speeds as a result of incomplete combustion.
- The internal combustion engine has a relatively flat torque-speed profile compared with an ideal one as shown. Therefore, a gearbox is usually employed to modify it as shown in Fig. 11.3.

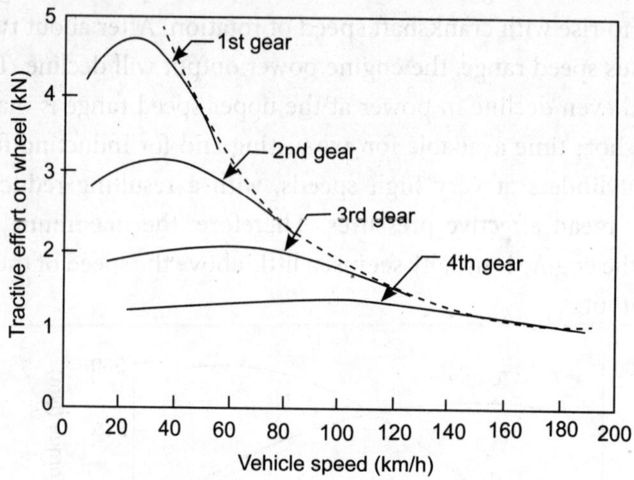

Fig. 11.3: Torque-speed profile

Characteristics of an Electric Motor at Full Load

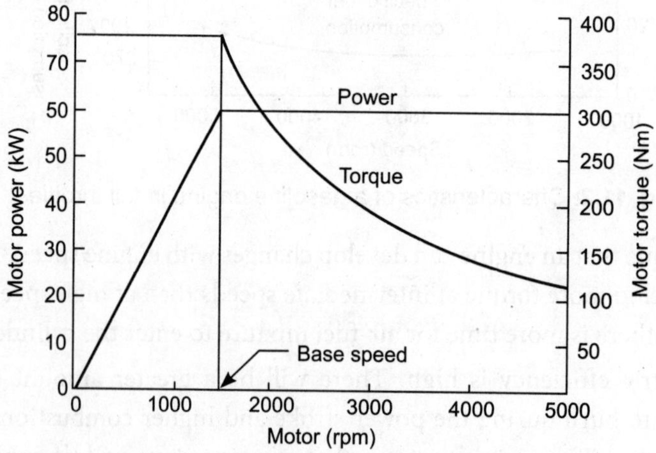

Fig. 11.4: Performance characteristics of electric motor as an automotive power plant

- Electric motors speed-torque characteristic is much closer to the ideal one.
- Generally, the electric motor starts from zero speed. As it increases to its base speed the voltage increases to its rated value while the flux remains constant. Beyond the base speed, the voltage remains constant and the flux is weakened. This results in constant output power while the torque declines hyperbolically with speed.
- Since the speed-torque profile of an electric motor is close to the ideal, a single gear or double gear gearbox is usually employed. Fig. 11.5 shows the tractive effort of a gasoline engine vehicle with four gear transmission and that of an electric vehicle with single-gear transmission. It is clear that electric machines with favorable torque–speed characteristics can satisfy tractive effort with simple single-gear transmission.

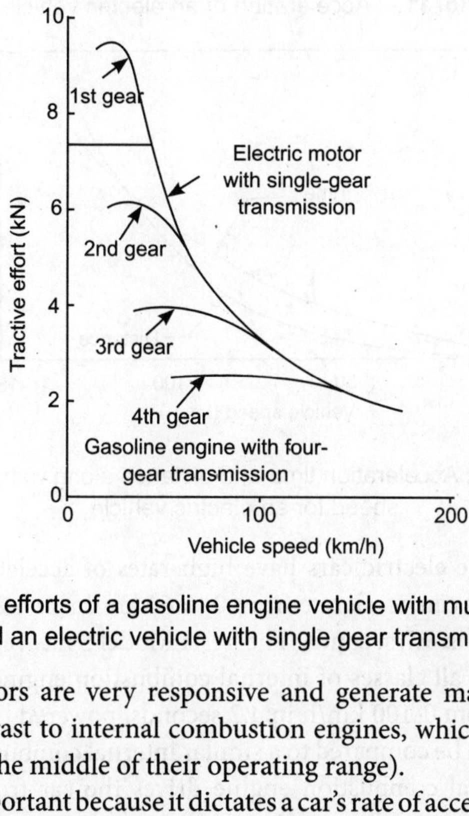

Fig. 11.5: Tractive efforts of a gasoline engine vehicle with multi gear transmission and an electric vehicle with single gear transmission

- Electric motors are very responsive and generate maximum torque from rest (in contrast to internal combustion engines, which generate maximum torque near the middle of their operating range).
- Torque is important because it dictates a car's rate of acceleration. Acceleration performance of a vehicle is evaluated by the time used to accelerate the vehicle from a low-speed (usually zero) to a higher speed (100 km/h for passenger cars). For passenger cars, acceleration performance is more important than maximum cruising speed and gradeability, since it is the acceleration requirement, rather than the maximum cruising speed or the gradeability, which dictates the power rating of the motor drive.

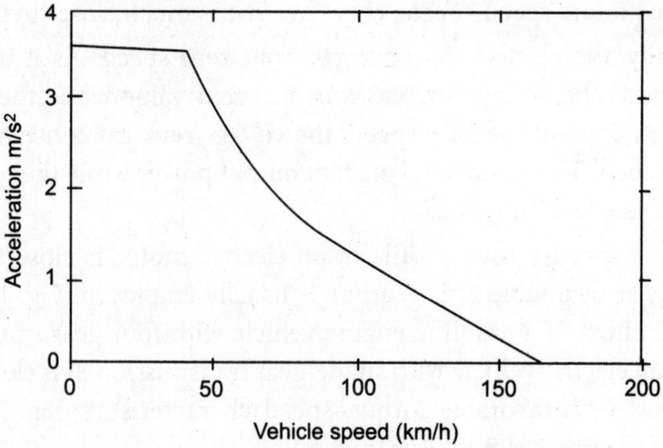

Fig. 11.6: Acceleration of an electric vehicle

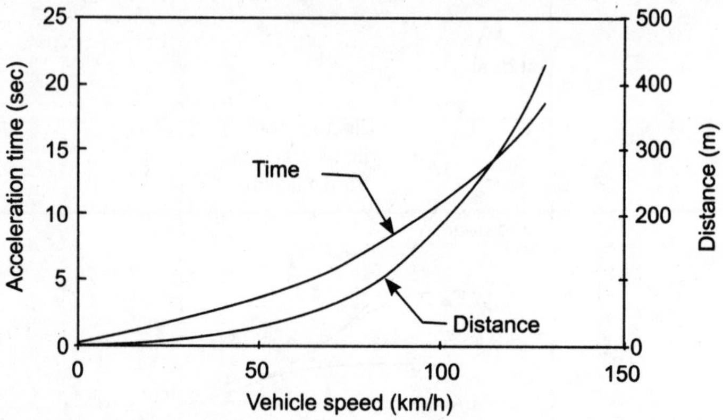

Fig. 11.7: Acceleration time and distance along with vehicle speed for an electric vehicle

- Even mid-range electric cars have high rates of acceleration; for example, the Nissan Leaf can accelerate from 0 to 60 km/hr in 4.2 seconds, and from 0 to 100 km/hr in 9.7 seconds. The Tesla Model S has very high acceleration compared with all classes of internal combustion engines, being capable of accelerating from 0-100 km/h in 4.2 seconds, powered by a 310 kW electric motor. This can be compared to a similar internal combustion engines whose 350 kW internal combustion engine drives the car from 0-100 km/hr in approximately 5 seconds.
- With a low centre of gravity and distributed weight of the batteries, EVs also offer better handling than internal combustion engines.
- Electric vehicles are much more energy efficient. Electric motors convert virtually all of their fuel energy into usable power. The internal combustion engine (ICE) is less than 20% efficient. Electric vehicles can be more efficient

than conventional vehicles, because electric motors are more efficient at low speeds unlike internal combustion engines, and because they do not use any power when coasting or at rest. Adding to the efficiency of battery-powered electric vehicles is the technique of regenerative braking.

REVIEW QUESTIONS

1. Draw the ideal performance characteristics graph for an automotive power plant.
2. Brief the performance characteristics of a gasoline engine in full throttle.
3. Discuss the torque-speed profile of a vehicle for various gear ratios.
4. Explain the performance characteristics of electric motoras an automotive power plant.

12 CHARGING

UNIT OUTCOMES

Upon successful completion of this module, the student will be able to:

1. Study the different types of chargers for EVs.
2. Get exposed to chargers for different locations

There are a range of options for charging electric cars, as described in the following sections. The average EV driver does 80 percent of their car charging at home. Different charging voltages and charger configurations can be used in charging the vehicles. Wireless charging is also being examined and experimented with to increase convenience.

Level 1 - Trickle Charge

EV can be plugged into any normal 220 V plug just like charging a mobile phone. This will add 8 km of range to EV per hour.

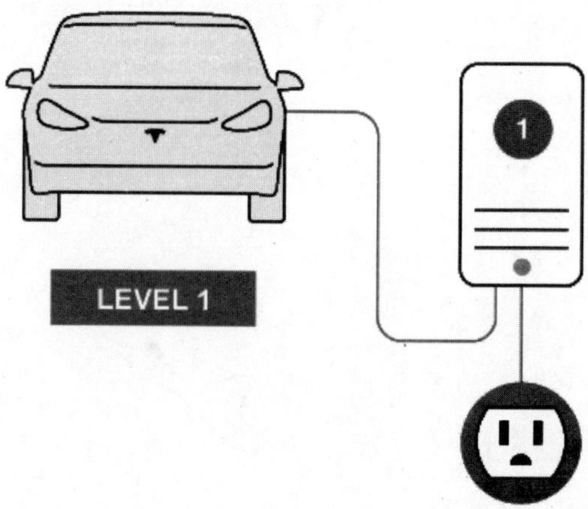

Fig. 12.1: Level 1 charging

Level 1 chargers are the least expensive electric vehicle supply equipment (EVSE) option, but they also take the most time to charge your car's battery. Homeowners typically use these types of chargers to charge their cars overnight.

Manufacturers of Level 1 EV chargers include AeroVironment, Duosida, Leviton, and Orion.

Level 2 - Charge at Home and Public Charging Station

Level 2 chargers are used for both residential and commercial charging stations. They use a 240 V (for residential) or 208 V (for commercial) plug, and unlike Level 1 chargers, they can't be plugged into a standard wall outlet. Instead, they are usually installed by a professional electrician. They can also be installed as part of a solar panel system.

Level 2 electric car chargers deliver 20 to 100 kms of range per hour of charging. They can fully charge an electric car battery in as little as two hours, making them an ideal option for both homeowners who need fast charging and businesses who want to offer charging stations to customers.

Many electric car manufacturers, like Nissan, have their own Level 2 charger products. Other Level 2 manufacturers include Clipper Creek, Chargepoint, Juice Box, and Siemens.

Home Charging

Most electric cars are likely to be charged at home when they are parked overnight. A single overnight charge is likely to be sufficient for the vast majority of users.

The most EV purchasers will install a 'Level 2' charger at home. A Level 2 charger operates at around 30 Amps and can charge much more rapidly than a standard electrical socket.

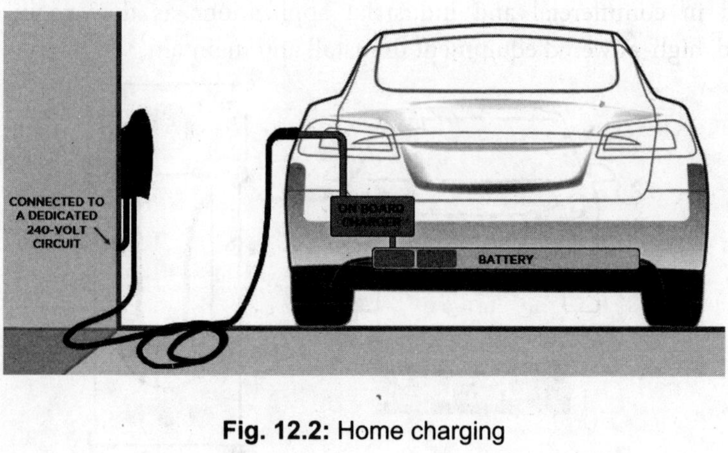

Fig. 12.2: Home charging

Public Charging

Public charging could be installed at any location where users typically park during the day, such as the workplace, shopping centres, public car parks, and on roadsides (via "bollards"). These would offer users the opportunity to "top-up" their charge level while they shop or go about their usual activities throughout the day, and would offer similar charge rates to home Level 2 chargers (around 100 km of charge in 3 hours, and a full re-charge of most recent model electric cars in around 4 hours). The use of these facilities may be offered free-of-charge to customers, or they may include payment facilities, depending upon the preference of the business, government or council installing and maintaining them.

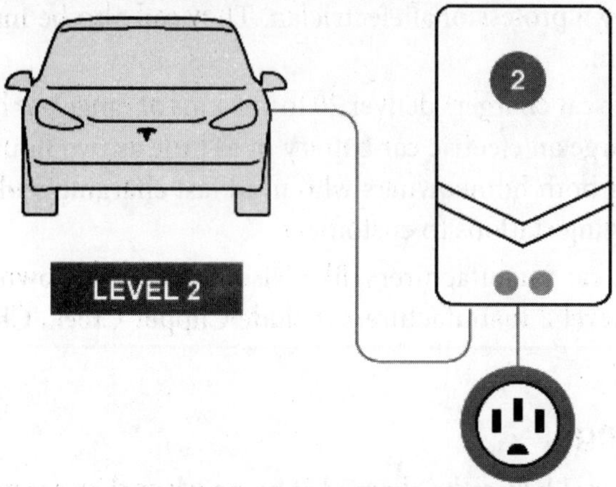

Fig. 12.3: Public charging

Level 3 - Fast Charge (High power stations)

Level 3 chargers, also known as DC Fast Chargers, offer the potential to recharge upto 80 percent of an electric car battery in 20 minutes. However, they are typically only used in commercial and industrial applications as they require highly specialised, high-powered equipment to install and maintain.

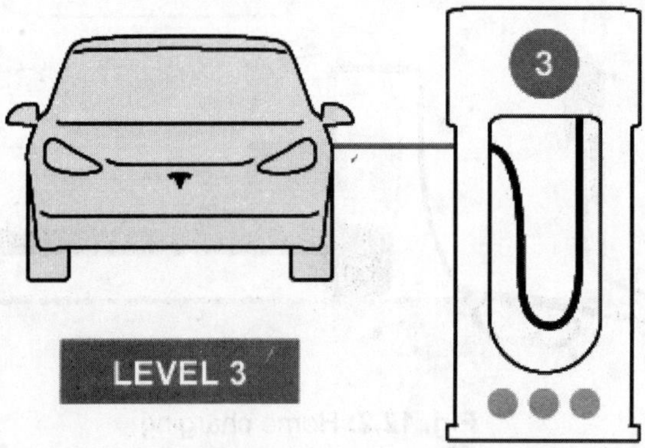

Fig. 12.4: Fast charging

It is also assumed that 10% of the charging infrastructure required in India shall be composed of fast charging station and rest 90% shall come from level 2 public charging set ups.

The Mitsubishi "i" and Nissan Leaf are two examples of electric cars that are DC Fast charger enabled.

Swap Station

Other models for charging have been proposed, such as swappable batteries. Electric cars could be designed such that upon driving into a swap station, the battery could be exchanged for a fully charged battery in two or three minutes (or less). The vehicle drives over a hatch at a charging station, and a robot removes and replaces the battery. This operation can be completely automated, such that the driver need not leave the vehicle.

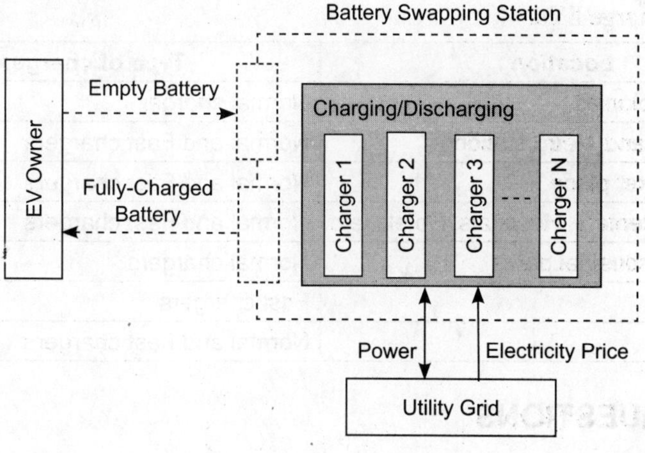

Fig. 12.5: Swap charging

Inductive Charging

Inductive charging may be another option in which charging occurs wirelessly. A charging pad is fixed to the ground under where the electric car parks and the electric car are fitted with receiving equipment under the chassis. No cables or plugs are required. A display screen on the wall in front of where the vehicle parks provide directional arrows to the driver when parking, to align the pad and receiver. The system is rated at 3.3 kW, which is sufficient to fully charge a Nissan Leaf from empty in approximately 8 hours. With an air gap of around 10 cm between pad and receiver, energy transfer rates of up to 90% can be achieved.

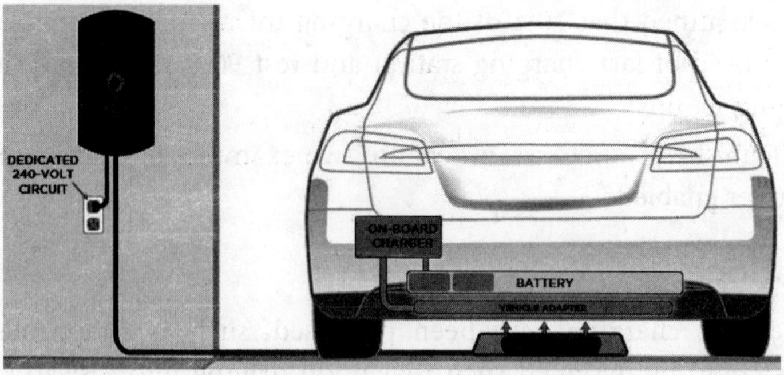

Fig. 12.6: Inductive charging

Locations and type of charger

The table below provides details about suitable types of chargers for different locations to charge EVs.

Location	Type of charger
Residential colonies	Normal charger
Railway, Bus and Metro stations	Normal and Fast chargers
Mall and Market place	Normal and Fast chargers
Commercial centers, Hospitals, Hotels, etc	Normal and Fast chargers
Techno and industrial parks	Normal chargers
Fuel station	Fast chargers
Highways	Normal and Fast chargers

REVIEW QUESTIONS

1. How are EV batteries charged?
2. What are the three main types of electric vehicle charging points?
3. What are EV charging standards?
4. How many EV charging stations are needed?
5. What is the cost of an EV charging station?
6. Can I charge my electric car at home?
7. How can I charge an electric car?
8. Can electric cars charge themselves?
9. How long does it take to charge an electric car?
10. How much does it cost to charge an electric car?
11. Write a note on swap station.
12. Brief about inductive charging.
13. What is the best way to charge an EV?
14. How do you calculate electric car charging time?

13 INDIAN ELECTRIC VEHICLES

UNIT OUTCOMES

Upon successful completion of this module, the student will be able to:

1. Get exposed to EVs on Indian roads.
2. Study the different types of EVs on Indian roads.

India is well suited for the introduction of EVs today with the existing technologies available, making EVs cost effective. EVs with a top speed of 40-60 kmph and a range of 50-60 km would meet over 90 percent of the city mobility requirements in India. The average daily driving distance for the metropolitan area in India is 35 kilometers, which is well within the range of typical electric cars.

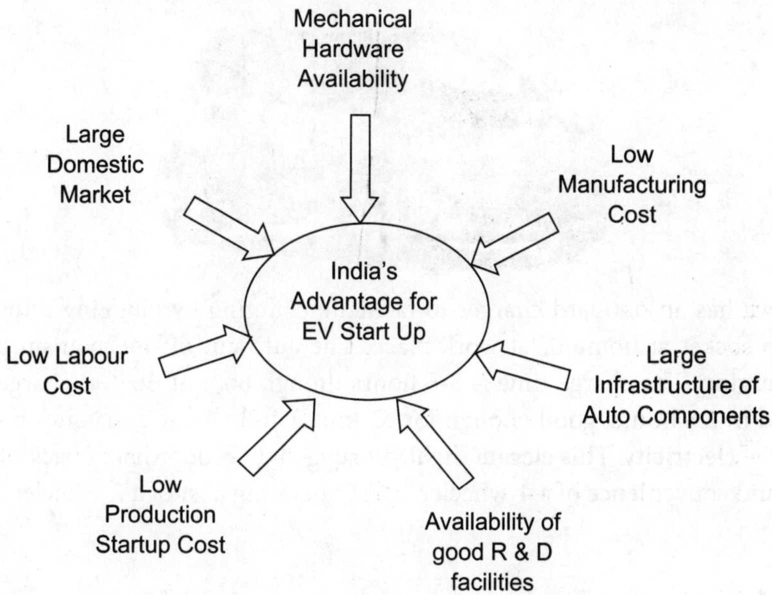

Fig. 13.1: India's advantages for EV start up

The current market for EVs is very small in India. Though there are different types of E2Ws (scooters and bikes), E4Ws (electric cars), and electric buses, the overall share of EVs is negligible.

India stands out for its mechanical hardware availability and low manufacturing cost. Other advantages for India are its low labour cost, low production start up cost, availability of R & D facilities in electrical, electronics and auo industries coupled with large infrastructure of auto components, less present investment in internal combustion engine capacity and the potential of large domestic markets. Information technology and electronics facilities further enhance its EV manufacturing potential. With the largest EV potential market in the world, the chance of reducing the production of EV costs in the near future is highest in India.

4-WHEELERS

REVA

The first electric car in India was launched by Bangalore based company REVA in early 2000s. Reva is a stylish, fully automatic (no clutch-no gears), compact two-door hatch back that carries two adults and two children or a payload of 227 kg. It has a top speed of 65 km/h and a range of 80 km. In view of traffic congestion, narrow roads and inadequate infrastructure characteristic of our Indian cities, the average driving speeds maintained during city driving are below 30 km/h. EVs like Reva are ideal for these conditions. A small turning radius of just 3.5 m makes it easy to park and maneuvers in difficult city traffic conditions.

Reva has an onboard charger to facilitate charging by plugging into a 220V, 15 amp socket at home or at work place. The auto cut-off mechanism prevents overcharging. The charge time is 5-6 hours though 80% of the full charge can be attained in 2.5 hours, good enough for 65 km. A full charge consumes just about 9 units of electricity. This elegant, light yet rugged, two-door hatch back offers the safety and convenience of a 4-wheeler at the operating cost of a 2-wheeler.

Mahindra Electric

Mahindra Electric Mobility Limited, formerly known as the Reva Electric Car Company, involved in designing and manufacturing of compact electric vehicles. Mahindra Electric started their journey in to the EV space in 2011 by launching Mahindra Reva, India's first electric car. They subsequently launched Mahindra E20, the current version on roads in India. Powered with Li-ion batteries, the new model allows for a top speed of 80 km/hr and a driving range of 100 km with a single charge. With a charging time of 5 hours, it is marketed to provide significant cost savings over a conventional car.

Tata motors

The list of Electric cars from Tata motors include Tata Nexon EV (₹ 13.99 Lakh, 2019), and Tata Tigor EV (₹ 10.58 Lakh, 2019).The Tigor Electric will be able to do about 120-150 kilometers on a full battery charge.

The Nano EV could be the first electric car that the automaker launches in India, followed by the Tigor and Tiago electric vehicles. Electric car charging infrastructure is at its infancy in India, and the government is fast stepping up its efforts to roll out charging stations.

Tata Motors is setting up 400 charging stations in Delhi alone and has plans for more cities. They plan to develop their own vendor for chargers as well.

Top Electric Cars in the Indian Market

1. Tata Nexon EV

With a 3 Phase Permanent Magnet Synchronous Motor (PMSM), the Nexon EV is one of the most impressive EV SUVs out there. Its Li-ion Polymer battery is equipped with liquid cooling to ensure that temperatures remain relatively low even after a long drive.

Even though it relies on electricity, this car can generate impressive peak powers of 127bhp.

- Battery capacity – 30.2 kWh
- Distance per charge – 312 km/full charge
- Recharge time – 0-80% charge in 60 minutes with a fast charger.
- Awards – Winner of Subcompact SUV of the Year Award at the 2018 edition of NDTV's Car and Bike Awards.
- Price – Starting from ₹13.99 lakh, 2019.

2. MG ZS EV

The British MG brand offers a premium EV, which counts as one of the top electric cars in India. It is powered by a similar motor like that in the Tata Nexon EV.

This impressively designed SUV boasts several brilliant features, including a 448-litre boot space, diamond-cut machined alloy wheels and power-assisted electric steering. It can also produce an immense torque of 353 Nm.

- Battery capacity – 44.5 kWh
- Distance per charge – 340 km/full charge
- Recharge time – Fast charging in 50 minutes. The normal charge takes 6-8 hours.
- Price – Starting from ₹ 20.88 lakh, 2019.

3. Tata Tigor EV

Powered by a three-phase AC induction motor, this electric sedan comes with max powers of 40 bhp along with peak torque of 105 Nm. The 310-litre boot space is an additional facility that can be very handy while storing luggage. Under ideal driving conditions, this car can reach speeds of 80 kmph.

- Battery capacity – 21.5 kWh
- Distance per charge – 142 km/full charge
- Recharge time – Fast charging in 90 minutes and normal charging in six hours.
- Price – Starting from ₹ 9.54 lakh, 2019.

4. Hyundai Kona Electric

Equipped with the advanced Permanent Magnet Synchronous Motor (PMSM), the Kona Electric is considered one of the best electric vehicles in India. It has a fierce pickup reaching 100 kmph in just under 10 seconds.

Along with its spectacular mileage, this car can produce immense torque at 395 Nm. Power-wise, the Kona Electric can generate around 134 bhp under ideal conditions.

- Battery capacity – 39.2 kWh
- Distance per charge – 452 km/full charge
- Recharge time – 57-minute fast charging and normal charging in six hours.
- Awards won – Winner of Electronic Vehicle of the Year Award at the 2019 Tech and Auto Awards.
- Price – Starting from ₹ 23.71 lakh, 2019.

5. Mahindra e2oPlus

A smaller body and a bevy of colour options are what define the e2oPlus from Mahindra. Although nowhere nearly as powerful as the electric SUVs in this list, it is perfect as a commute vehicle. Its 3-phase, AC Induction Motor is equipped with a Li-ion battery, weighing 84 kg.

It can generate maximum torque and power of 70 Nm and 25 bhp, respectively.

- Battery capacity – 10.08 kWh
- Distance per charge – 99.9 km/full charge
- Recharge time – 75 minutes with a fast charger and six hours with a standard charger.
- Price – Starting from ₹ 7.57 lakh, 2019.

6. Mahindra e-Verito

Another Mahindra offering, the e-Verito is a sedan, unlike the e2oPlus. It is equipped with a similar AC-induction, three-phase motor. However, this vehicle offers an immense boot space, around 510-litre, which makes it perfect for hauling large bags and equipment.

Additional features include an electro-hydraulic power steering and tubeless steel wheels.

- Battery capacity – 21.2 kWh
- Distance per charge – 140 km/full charge
- Recharge time – Fast charging in 1 hour and 45 minutes.
- Price – Starting from ₹ 10.11 lakh, 2019.

3-WHEELERS

More recently, electric rickshaws are gaining popularity as a good substitute for conventional three-wheelers (rickshaws) and paddle-rickshaws as public and goods transportation over short-to-medium distances. Scooters India Ltd and Mahindra & Mahindra Ltd have brought out battery operated three wheelers, which are already running in several cities in India. Bajaj, TVS and Ashok Leyland are working on hybrid and pure electric EVs.

In Delhi alone there are more than 100,000 e-rickshaws. e-rickshaws must be registered and the drivers are required to have driving licenses.

The challenges for using e-rickshaws are:

1. Use of lead-acid batteries, which need to be replaced within 7-8 months.
2. Current design of e-rickshaws does not possess the required vehicle strength and often fail on safety standards.
3. Unavailability of fixed e-rickshaws stands and charging points.

2-WHEELERS

2-Wheeler is the largest segment in the Indian automotive industry representing ~80% of Indian automotive sales. Around the year 2000, only a couple of electric two-wheelers were available in the Indian market. However, the market has expanded and over two dozen different two-wheelers are available in the market at present. These include low speed vehicles with a maximum speed of 25 km/hr to high speed vehicles capable of achieving speeds up to 115 km/hr. The driving range varies from 20 km to 150 km.

The following aspects would help drive e-mobility in this segment:

- Over 2 million petrol-run delivery bikes with a long daily run engaged in courier and food delivery services.
- Intra-city travels (maximum of around 100-150 km a day)
- Ease of charging: Can be easily charged on a standard residential/workplace plug point.

	e-Bike	Petrol run Bike
Range, km	70 – 120	300 – 450
Price, ₹	90,000 – 1,25,000	75,000 – 1,20,000

Top electric motorcycles and scooters in the Indian market

Here is a list of the best electric bikes in India.

1. Revolt RV 400

The Revolt RV400 is the first AI-enabled electric motorcycle in the Indian market. The Revolt RV 400 electric motorcycle is offered in two variants: Standard and premium and has a maximum 150 km on a single charge. Both motorcycles offer a host of features, AI-enabled technology and unique payment and maintenance schemes.

2. Ultraviolette F77

The Ultraviolette F77 electric motorcycle draws its design inspiration from the aviation space. The motorcycle sports a modern look and sure to be head-turner when seen on the streets. Internet connectivity, smartphone application, fully-digital instrument cluster, ABS, regenerative braking and more. The motorcycle houses three batteries of 4.2 kWh each paired with an electric motor producing 33.5 bhp and 90 Nm of torque. The power is sent to rear wheels via a chain-drive set-up. The company claims the F77 can reach 0 to 100 kmph in 2.9 seconds and carry on to reach a top speed of 147 kmph. The Ultraviolette F77 features 150 km riding range from on a single charge from its 3 batteries. It also features fast charging that can take the batteries from 0 to 80 percent in 50 minutes.

3. Hero Electric Dash

The Hero Electric Dash looks modern and is wider in profile compared to most electric scooters. The electric scooter features, LED headlamps, LED DRLs, remote boot opening, USB charging port, large seat, and a 145mm ground clearance. The Hero Electric Dash is powered by a 48 V 28 Ah Li-ion battery, paired with a 250 W motor. The electric scooter offers a claimed range of 60 km on a single charge. The Dash features fast-charging technology with charging times rated at 4 hours for a full charge.

4. Bajaj Chetak

The Bajaj Chetak electric is the most luxurious electric scooter in the country. Bajaj Chetak electric is propelled by a 3-kWh Li-ion battery pack which delivers a range of about 85 to 95 km in a full charge.

Hence, there is no fast charging facility available on the Chetak and one has to wait full 5 hours before the battery can be fully charged. However, the 80% charge is completed in 3.5 hours which makes it quite practical is case of immediate requirements.

A 3800 Watts BLDC motor with a peak power of 4080 Watts is what makes the Chetak moves. The top speed of Bajaj Chetak is 78 kmph which is idle for city use.

5. TVS iQube

TVS iQube is a funky electric scooter with futuristic design language. It gets a 4.5 kWh Li-ion battery pack which is IP67 certified for being water-resistant. Despite having a large 4.5 kWh battery, the scooter runs for a mileage 75 km in the Eco mode which is the downside of the iQube.

With a 4400 Watts electric motor, the TVS iQube can touch a top speed of 78 kmph which is enough for daily rides.

6. Ampere Magnus Pro

Ampere is an electric vehicle manufacturer and it is fast gaining its market share in the tier 2 and tier 3 cities of the country. The company is catering mostly to the rural areas as their electric bikes are sturdy and can handle the bad terrain of the rural areas.

Magnus Pro is equipped with a small 1.8 kWh Li-ion battery pack which can deliver a real-world range between 75-80 km. The battery charges in 5-6 hours which is more than that of Hero Photon's charging time.

The hub mounted BLDC motor has power rating of 1200 Watts which allows to hit 40 kmph from zero in 10 seconds. Magnus Pro has a top speed of 55 kmph. These performance numbers suggest that scooter is well suited for customers in tier 2 and tier 3 cities as well as in rural areas.

ELECTRIC BUS

The Bangalore Municipal Transport Corporation has recently introduced an electric bus on a dense corridor in the city.

Intra-city buses are likely to be electrified early, driven by the support provided by government-run transport undertakings, route predictability and ease of charging at bus depots.

E-TRUCKS

The demand for fuel-efficient trucks is expected to increase further with India's plan to leapfrog to BS-VI emission norms in 2020. This could provide a thrust toward the adoption of electric trucks in India as ICE trucks are likely to get costlier by up to 20%, leading to a convergence in prices of diesel-powered and e-trucks.

REVIEW QUESTIONS

1. List the India's advantages for EVs start up.
2. What are the challenges to introduce EVs in 3-wheelers?
3. What is the first EV in India?
4. Who is the major seller of EVs in India?
5. List out the top electric cars in Indian market.

14 HYBRID VEHICLES

UNIT OUTCOMES

Upon successful completion of this module, the student will be able to:

1. Study the different types of HEVs.
2. Differentiate HEVs from EVs and ICEs.
3. Explain the components of HEVs.

Pure electric vehicles run only on batteries and need a charger to replenish the battery's power from an electrical outlet.

A hybrid is a vehicle that has two or more power sources to propel it. An example that is often seen is a moped. The petrol engine is one power source and the rider provides the second power source by 'pedal power'. Other vehicles that are classed as hybrid include some trains (diesel and electric) and submarines (nuclear and electric).

HYBRID ELECTRIC VEHICLES (HEV)

A hybrid electric vehicle (HEV) is a type of vehicle that uses both an electric motor (s) and a conventional internal combustion engine (petrol or diesel engine). This type of vehicle is considered to have better performance (increased torque and power), fuel economy and reduced emissions compared to a conventional one of the same size, performance and comfort.

Hybrid vehicle has a smallbattery (shown in red color) which drives the vehicle over a short distance before switching to engine. A hybrid electric vehicle cannot be plugged in for charging. Instead, the battery is charged through regenerative braking and by the internal combustion engine

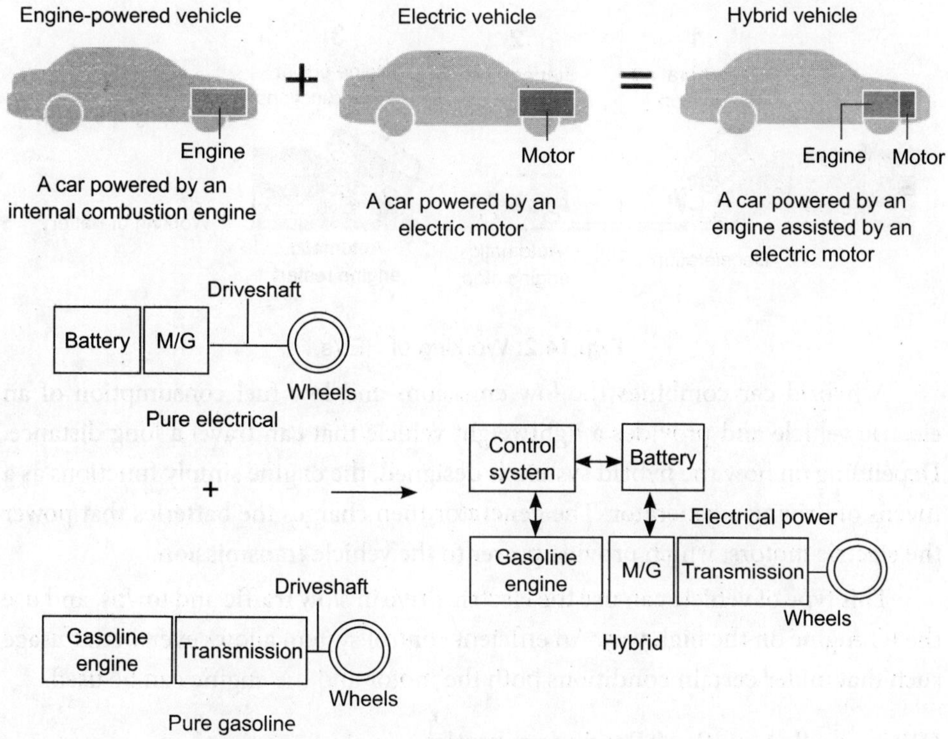

Fig. 14.1: Concept of Hybrid Electric Vehicle

Hybrid electric vehicles (HEVs) incorporate a small internal combustion engine with an electric motor and storage batteries. They eliminate the basic weaknesses of electric vehicles (limited range; bulky and heavy, more time for recharge, etc) and internal combustion engines (harmful emissions, higher fuel consumption, etc).

A hybrid electric vehicle has more promise than an electric vehicle, since the HEV has an internal combustion engine to provide the energy to meet vehicle range requirements. The battery then provides the additional power needed for acceleration and climbing hills. The fuels used in the HEV engines in current production include gasoline, diesel and natural gas.

Internal combustion (IC) engines produce dangerous emissions and have poor efficiency at part load. IC engine cars are both lightweight and can cover extensive distances before they need to refill the fuel tank. Refilling the fuel tank is very rapid compared with the time taken to recharge batteries. The disadvantages of the IC engines are high emissions and high fuel consumption when compared to electric power.Electric drives produce 'no' emissions but have a limited range. The solution is to combine the best aspects of both IC engine and electric drives.

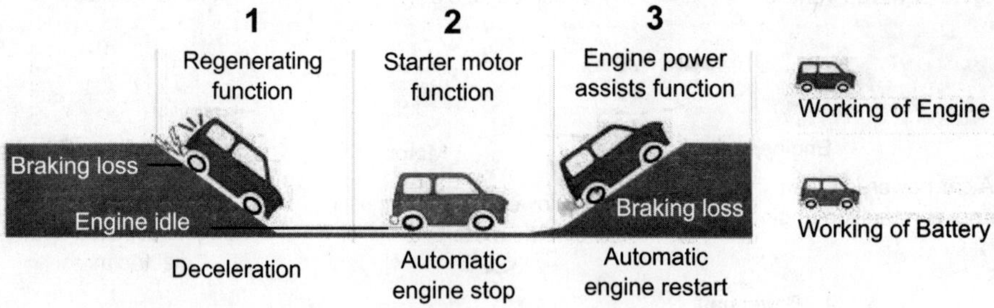

Fig. 14.2: Working of HEVs

A hybrid car combines the low emissions and low fuel consumption of an electric vehicle and provides a lightweight vehicle that can travel a long distance. Depending on how the hybrid system is designed, the engine simply functions as a means of driving a generator. The generator then charges the batteries that power the electric motors, which provide power to the vehicle transmission.

This type of vehicle can use the electric drive in slow traffic and towns, and use the IC engine on the high way. An efficient control system allows even better usage such that under certain conditions both the motor and the engine can be used.

HEVs usually have the following properties

1. Auto-start/auto-shutdown - To avoid wasting energy during idle time, the engine of a hybrid electric vehicle automatically shuts down and starts as soon as the accelerator is touched.
2. Regenerative braking - Considered one of the salient features of HEVs, the energy wasted during braking and coasting is converted and stored in the battery, which is then used by the electric motor.
3. Electric motor assist - By helping the engine during passing, accelerating or moving up a hill, the electric motor allows the engine to be made smaller and more efficient in nature.

Advantages

1. Low exhaust emission levels.
2. Longer range than BEV.
3. Engines can be down sized to accommodate average load, not peak load, which reduces the engine's weight.
4. Fuel efficiency is greatly increased.
5. Low maintenance cost

Disadvantages

1. Bulky and heavy.
2. Require very complicated control systems.
3. Still produces emissions
4. Expensive to operate (8-10 times more expensive than BEV) but less than traditional gasoline vehicle.
5. No ability to conveniently charge at home.

COMPONENTS OF HYBRID ELECTRIC VEHICLE

A typical hybrid car contains the following components.

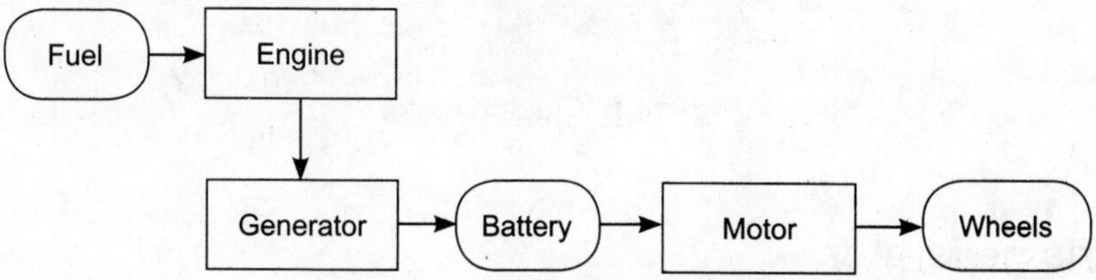

Fig. 14.3: Components of HEVs

Petrol engine

The engine is similar to those fitted to conventional vehicles e.g. four cylinders, four-stroke normally aspirated, etc. However, the capacity of the engine used is usually relatively small. These engines are lightweight and very fuel efficient. They typically produce approximately 70 brake horsepower which is supplemented with a electric motor rated typically at approximately 50 horse power.

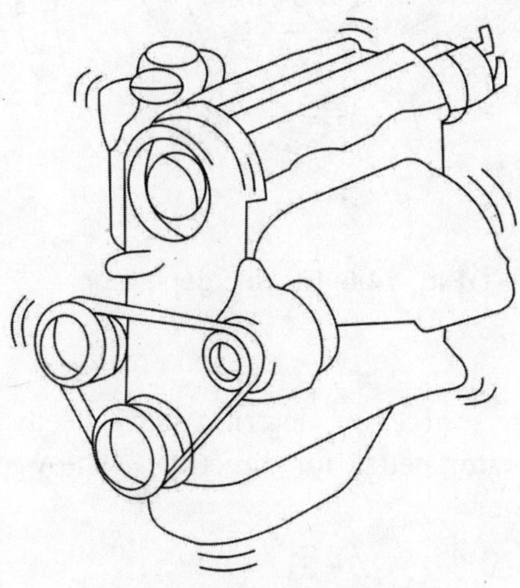

Fig. 14.4: Petrol engine

Electric motor

The electric motor is used to propel the car, however with the use of electronic technology, the motor can also function as a generator to recharge the batteries.

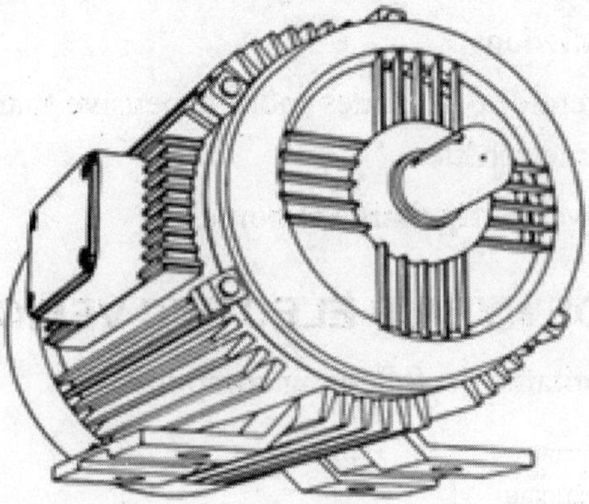

Fig. 14.5: Electric motor

Electric generator

Electric generator generates electricity from the rotating wheels while braking, transferring that energy back to the traction battery pack. Some vehicles use motor generators that perform both the drive and regeneration functions.

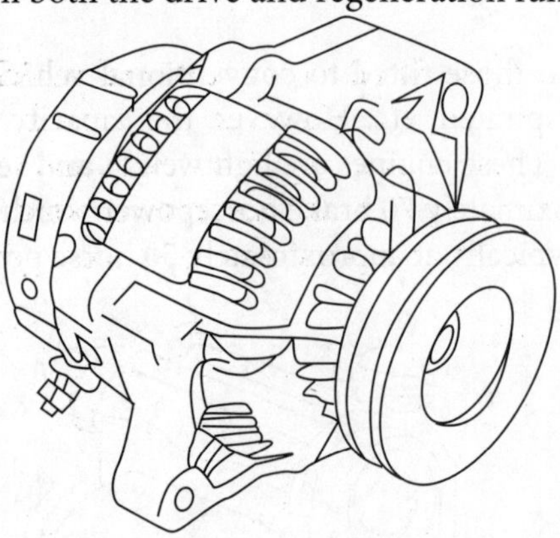

Fig. 14.6: Electric generator

Controller

Regardless of the energy source, an electric vehicle needs a controller, which is connected to the accelerator pedal, for directing the flow of electricity from the energy source to the motor.

DC/DC converter

This device converts higher-voltage DC power from the traction battery pack to the lower-voltage DC power needed to run vehicle accessories and recharge the auxiliary battery.

Transmission

The transmission transfers mechanical power from the engine and/or electric traction motor to drive the wheels. The transmission can be either manual or automatic.

Fig. 14.7: Transmission

Fuel tank

The fuel tank is used to store petrol for the petrol engine.

Batteries

The batteries provide the energy source for the electric motor, either recharged by an external power source or recharged by the generator or electric motor when it is functioning as a generator. Most electric cars use lead-acid batteries, but new types of batteries, including zinc-chlorine, nickel metal-hydride and sodium-sulphur, are becoming more common.

Battery (auxiliary)

In an electric drive vehicle, the auxiliary battery provides electricity to start the car before the traction battery is engaged and also powers vehicle accessories.

Traction battery pack

Traction battery pack stores electricity for use by the electric traction motor.

WORKING OF HYBRID VEHICLES

Figs. 14.8-14.11 show the energy flows in a basic HEV.

Starting

While starting the vehicle, the IC engine may run the motor as a generator to produce some power and store it in the battery.

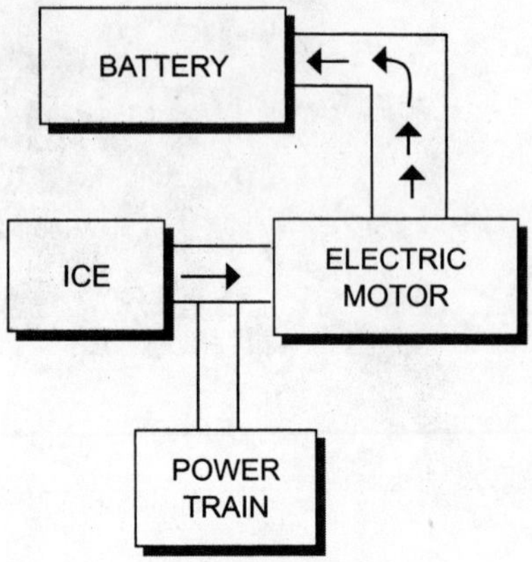

Fig. 14.8: Starting

Passing

Passing needs a boost in speed, therefore the IC engine and the motor both drives the power train.

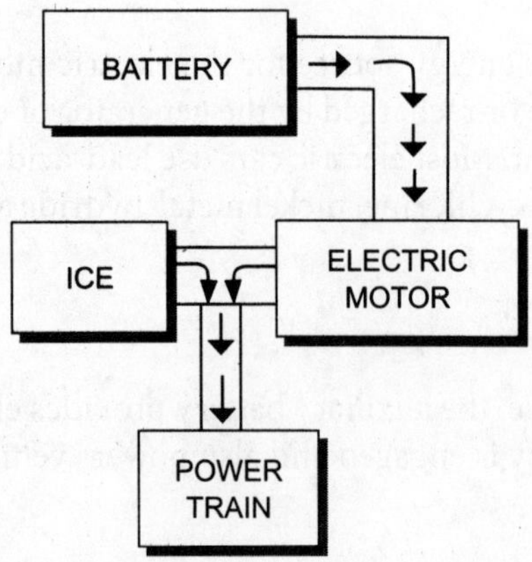

Fig. 14.9: Passing

Braking

During braking the power train runs the motoras generator to charge the battery by regenerative braking.

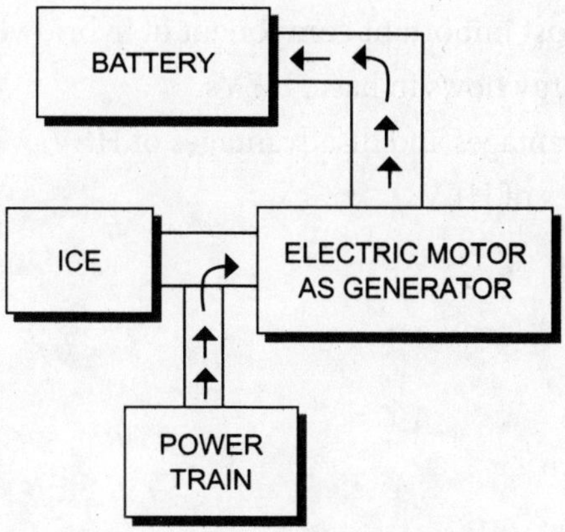

Fig. 14.10: Braking

Cruising

While cruising, IC engine runs both the vehicle and the motor as generator, which charges the battery. The power flow is stopped once the vehicle stops.

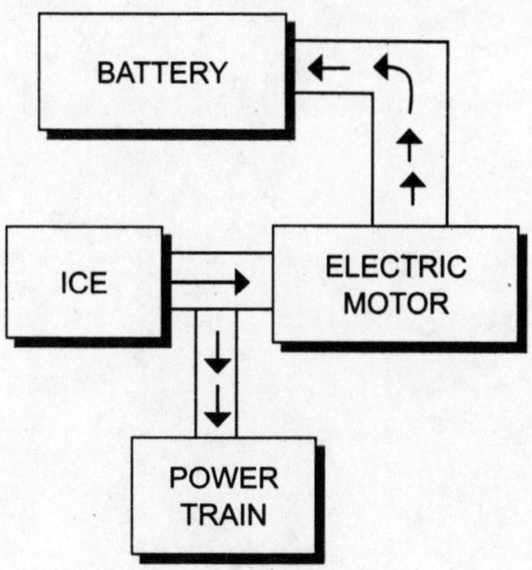

Fig. 14.11: Cruising

REVIEW QUESTIONS

1. What is hybrid electric vehicle?
2. What challenges do hybrid electric vehicles face?
3. What makes hybrid electric vehicles special?
4. What are the main components of hybrid electric vehicle?
5. Which is the most important component of hybrid vehicle?
6. Discuss the energy flows in basic HEVs.
7. List out the advantages and disadvantages of HEVs.
8. Brief the features of HEVs.

15 HYBRIDISATION

UNIT OUTCOMES

Upon successful completion of this module, the student will be able to:

1. Classify the hybridisation.
2. Identify the types of mild hybrids.
3. Fabricate HEVs

Hybrid cars are most commonly classified in following three categories:

1. Micro hybrid
2. Mild hybrid
3. Full hybrid

MICRO HYBRID

Micro hybrid technology is the lowest level of vehicle hybridisation. It contains mainly start stop technology. Here, energy stored in an auxiliary battery is used to quickly start a vehicle at the traffic signal.

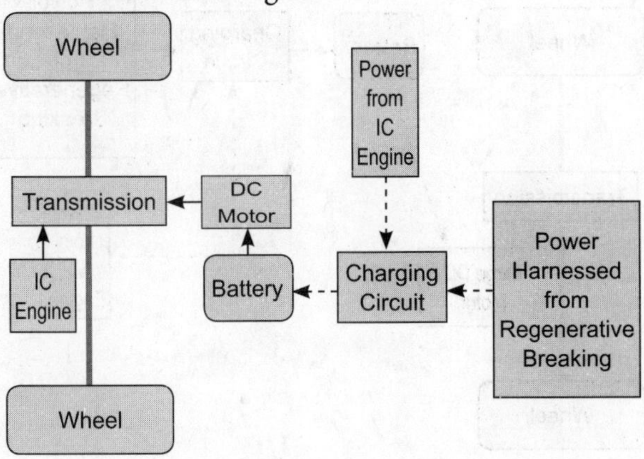

Fig. 15.1: Block diagram of a micro hybrid

In this system the starter and the alternator are replaced with an electrical machine. The internal combustion engine switched off when the vehicle stops. When the vehicle sets off again it is quietly accelerated to idle speed by the electrical machine, and then the ignition is activated.

Advantages

1. Fuel consumption is reduced from 5 to 10% in city driving.
2. CO_2 emission is reduced.
3. Engine restarts in milliseconds.
4. Noise and vibrations are suppressed.
5. Implementation cost is not very high.

Disadvantages

1. High maintenance cost
2. Some vehicle functions (air conditioner, etc) may not run when engine is off.

Application

In India, a common example of micro hybrid is the Mahindra Scorpio. Tata motors introduced this technique in Tata ACE. BMW, Fiat, Honda, Volkswagon and many other automobile manufacturers use this technology.

MILD HYBRID

The next level of hybridisation is the mild hybrid where electrical energy is used for start stop and also for driving vehicle for short distance at low speed or to aid in acceleration. A mild hybrid's motor is only able to assist the engine; it is not potent enough to drive the car independently, hence the word 'mild'.

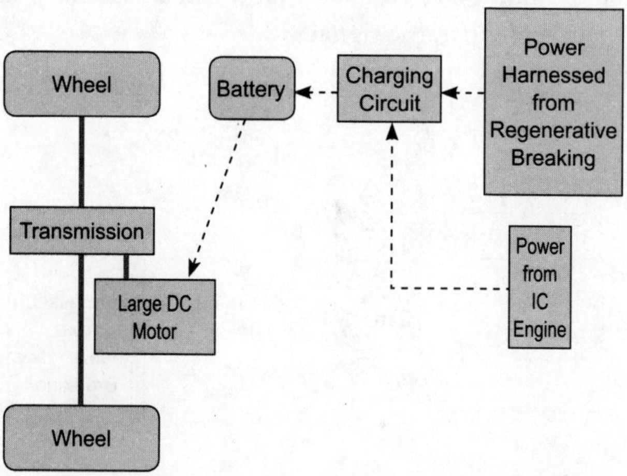

Fig. 15.2: Block diagram of a series mild hybrid

Mild hybrid cars spend most of their time powered by their combustion engine, with a small motor/generator usually taking the place of a conventional alternator – the device that normally charges the battery in a regular combustion-engined car. The electric motor can be directly flanged to the crankshaft in a mild hybrid. In mild hybrids, additional electrical energy of up to 20 kW is provided by the electric traction accumulator (battery). Unlike a full hybrid system the electric motor of a mild-hybrid system never propels the car on its own, with the motor/generator only delivering power for starting off and accelerating at low engine rpm.

As well as providing a boost to the engine, mild hybrids cut the ignition when engine power isn't needed such as when stationary, rolling or when braking – a system more commonly known as engine start-stop. Some also capture energy using regenerative braking, which converts the car's kinetic energy when decelerating and stores it as electrical energy in the batteries.

Advantages

1. Improve efficiency by up to 15%
2. Weight savings
2. Smoother starting

Disadvantages

1. Not able to run on electric power alone.
2. Higher CO_2 emissions than conventional hybrids

Applications

Honda Insight, Honda CR-Z.

Types of Mild hybrid

Mild hybrid is of two types:

1. Parallel mild hybrid
2. Series mild hybrid

Parallel Mild Hybrid

A small DC motor (Starter/generator) is coupled in parallel with the main IC engine. The additional DC motor provides assistance to the IC engine as and when required. The DC motor makes use of the battery which utilized the regenerative braking system power for charging. It also uses intelligent Stop-Start system. It cannot power the vehicle with DC motor alone.

Example: General Motors Parallel Hybrid Truck

Series Mild Hybrid

Here a large DC motor is coupled directly with the wheels. The motor is charged by an IC engine with additional support from the power harnessed from the other sources. It also uses intelligent Stop-Start system. Here the vehicle can be run by the DC motor alone.

Example: Chevy Malibu

FULL HYBRID

A full hybrid (HEV), sometimes also called a strong hybrid, is driven over longer distances with the electric drive alone. The internal combustion engine does not function during electric driving. As strong hybrids can travel considerable distance using electrical energy only, zero emissions can be achieved. The accumulator of these systems is more powerful than those of the above-mentioned micro-hybrid and mild-hybrid variants. The voltage of the traction electrical system or the battery usually ranges between 200 and 350V. It has a typical output of about 25 to 50 kW.

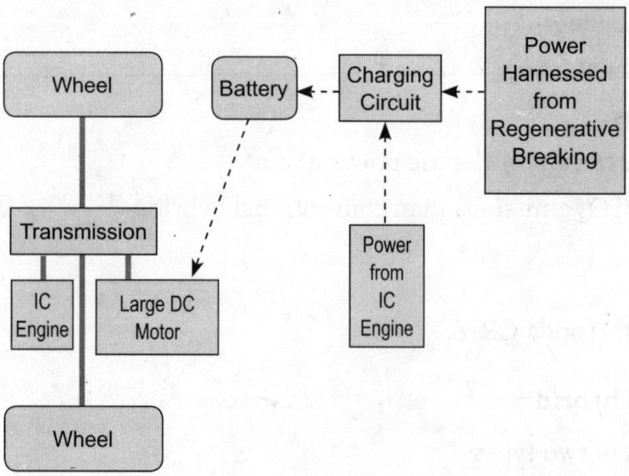

Fig. 15.5: Block diagram of a full hybrid

The full hybrid can be classified as a parallel hybrid or a series hydrid. The fuel savings of a full hybrid can be up to 30%.

Example: Lexus CT200h

START-STOP SYSTEM

Both mild-hybrid and strong-hybrid systems have a start/stop function. The Start Stop system is based on a simple principle of not burning the fuel when it is not required. When the vehicle is stopped, the engine ECU checks whether

- gears are in neutral
- speed sensor in ABS indicates zero
- battery sensor indicates sufficient energy for a starting

When these conditions are satisfied, the engine is automatically switched off. Thus it aids in attaining better fuel efficiency and reducing running costs. The working of this system as follows:

- Vehicle has come to halt due to traffic signal/jam, is in neutral gear.
- The engine will shut down automatically after 10 seconds. Just before stopping, the indicator in the cluster will blink indicating the engine is going to stop shortly.
- The indicator will glow on ~~your~~ instrument cluster indicating the engine has stopped due to stop start device.
- Once the signal turns green, press the clutch pedal and engine starts immediately.

The indicator on the cluster goes off indicating that engine has started again and ready to drive on with the vehicle. Fuel savings of 3.5-4.5% can be achieved by the start/stop system.

REVIEW QUESTIONS

1. What is micro hybrid?
2. What are the merits and demerits of mild hybrid?
3. What is mild hybrid?
4. List the merits and demerits of mild hybrid.
5. Classify the mild hybrid.
6. Differentiate series mild hybrid from parallel mild hybrid.
7. What is strong hybrid?
8. Give the importance of start-stop system.

16 DRIVE CONFIGURATIONS OF HEVs

UNIT OUTCOMES

Upon successful completion of this module, the student will be able to:

1. Study the drive configuration of HEVs.
2. Get exposed to control strategies for HEVs.

The HEV can be classified by the way in which the electrical and internal combustion engine (gasoline or diesel) components are combined and interconnected. The two power sources are combined either in parallel or in series. A design which combines both hybrids is known as a split-power hybrid.

SERIES HYBRID

The power sources are connected in series (Fig. 16.1), hence the name series hybrid. In a series configuration only the electric motor with power from the battery or generator is used to drive the wheels. The internal combustion engine is not connected to the drive. The engine never drives the car, it only produces energy for the electric motor. The internal combustion engine is maintained at its most efficient and lowest emission operating points to run the generator and charge the storage batteries. All of the energy that is needed to move the vehicle is therefore transmitted to the drive shaft by the electric motor.

This type of hybrid is also referred to as range extender hybrid.

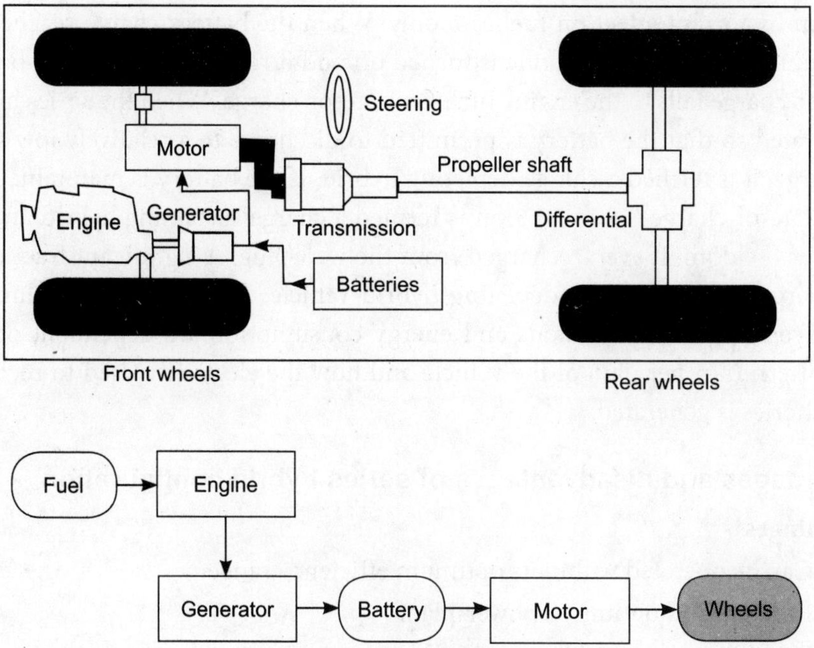

Fig. 16.1: Series hybrid

Applications

Buses (Toyota Coaster) and Diesel trains. The BMW i3 with Range Extender is one of the most popular examples. The Honda Jazz Hybrid also uses an electric motor to help their relatively small conventional engines when required.

Control strategies for series hybrid vehicles

The purpose of the control strategy is to maintain the state-of-charge of the energy storage unit within a prescribed range regardless of the driving cycle and the resultant power demand on the driveline. This should be done so that the onboard electrical generator (engine/generator or fuel cell) is operated at high efficiency and low emissions. This is done more easily when the energy storage capacity is reasonably large as with a battery than when it is small as using ultracapacitors.

The strategy used for vehicles having a significant all-electric range is to discharge the battery to a prescribed state-of-charge (20 to 30%) and then to turn on the engine to maintain the battery within 10 to 20 percent of that condition. Electrical energy is generated at a rate slightly greater than the average power demand of the vehicle to account for losses associated with storing the energy. In the case of an engine/generator, a minimum power level is set so that the engine is never operated below it. Proper selection of this minimum power can have an important effect on fuel economy. When the battery charge reaches the maximum permitted, the engine is turned off and it remains off until the battery state-of-charge falls to the engine turn-on state-of-charge. When the series hybrid is operated so that the battery is permitted to discharge to a relatively low state-of-charge, it is termed a charge depleting hybrid. If the battery is maintained at a high state-of-charge (60 to 70%), it is termed a charge sustaining hybrid and the battery is seldom, if ever, recharged from the wall-plug. A significant fraction of the energy used by charge depleting hybrid vehicles is from the wall-plug and their average annual emissions and energy consumption are dependent on the use-pattern (km per day) of the vehicle and how the electricity used to recharge the batteries is generated.

Advantages and disadvantages of series hybrid configuration

Advantages

1. Can be operated within its optimum efficiency range.
2. Efficient and optimised power-plant
3. Possibilities for modular power-plant
4. Optimised drive line
5. Possibility of swift 'black box' service exchange
6. Long lifetime
7. Mature technology
8. Fast response
9. Capable of attaining zero emission

Disadvantages

1. Large traction drive system
2. Requirement of proper algorithms
3. Multiple energy conversion steps
4. About 30% total loss of efficiency is observed due to multiple energy conversions.

PARALLEL HYBRID

These are the most common type of hybrid. The car's wheels can be powered in three different ways: either directly by the engine, by the electric motor alone, or by both power sources working together. In a parallel hybrid electric vehicle the single electric motor and the internal combustion engine are installed to deliver power in parallel to drive the wheels. As both the engine and electric motor are connected to the drive shaft through a mechanical coupling, they can propel the vehicle by the engine alone, by the motor alone, or by both together. The electric motor can be used as a generator to charge the energy storage devices (battery or ultra-capacitors) by regeneration braking or by extra power from the engine.

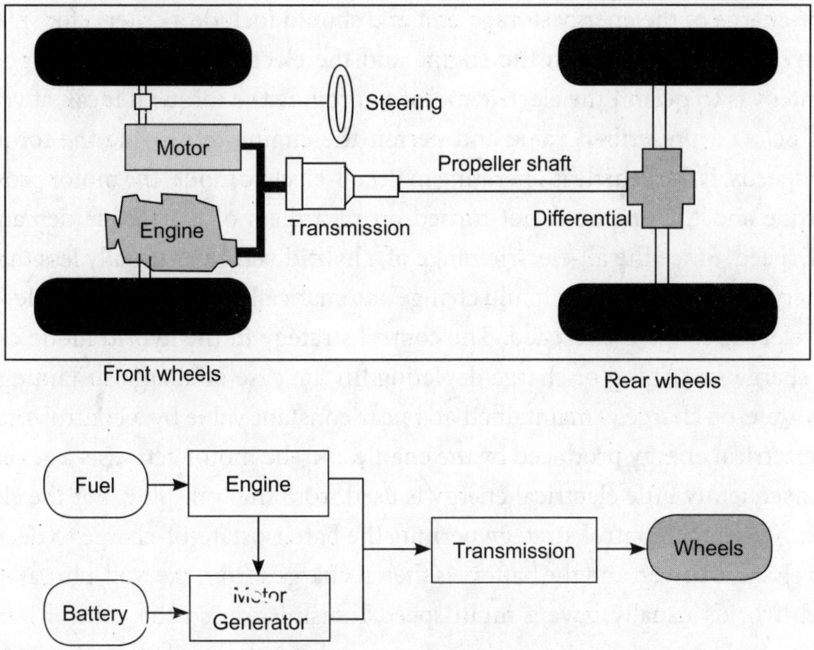

Fig. 16.2: Parallel hybrid

As the engine is connected to the wheels via mechanical coupling, it makes this type hybrid quite efficient on the highway. In addition, a parallel hybrid vehicle only needs two propulsion devices – engine and electric motor, which makes the system very compact.

The result is that a parallel hybrid has fewer components than a series hybrid, which makes the system more cost effective.

The battery is big enough that the electric motor can power the car for up to 200 kms.

Parallel hybrid with an electric motor fixed to the crankshaft

This parallel hybrid uses the internal combustion engine as its main energy source. The electric motor is used for assistance during acceleration.

Parallel hybrid with electric power only

In the parallel hybrid that can use electric power only, the electric motor is used more frequently and the engine less frequently.

Control strategies for parallel hybrid vehicles

The control strategies for parallel hybrid vehicles are more complicated than those for series hybrids primarily because they are dependent on both vehicle speed and state-of-charge of the energy storage unit and should include a criteria for splitting the driveline torque between the engine and the electric motor. The purpose of the strategy is to permit the electric motor to provide the torque if it can at vehicle speeds below a prescribed value and permit the engine to provide the torque at higher speeds. If the vehicle is operating in the all-electric mode, the motor provides the torque and the engine is not turned on regardless of the torque demand or vehicle speed. Since the all-electric range of a hybrid vehicle is usually less than 80 km, operation of the vehicle should change automatically to the hybrid mode when the all-electric range is exceeded. The control strategy in the hybrid mode can be either charge sustaining or charge depleting. In the case of charge sustaining, the battery state-of-charge is maintained at a near constant value by a control strategy using electrical energy produced by the engine and the motor acting as a generator and consequently little electrical energy is used from the wall-plug. For the charge depleting case, the control strategy permits the battery state-of-charge to decrease as the vehicle is driven and the battery is then recharged from the wall-plug at night. Parallel hybrids usually have a multi-speed transmission so the control strategy must also include a gear shifting algorithm that depends on whether the motor or engine or both are producing torque. A continuously variable transmission (CVT) would be particularly attractive for use in a parallel hybrid driveline.

In order to achieve high fuel economy with a parallel hybrid, it is necessary to avoid engine operation below some minimum engine torque (or effective throttle setting) where the engine brake specific fuel consumption (gm/kWh) is relatively high and to manage engine turn on and off carefully to minimize emissions and wasted fuel. In urban driving, the control strategies for parallel hybrids often result in the engine being turned on and off frequently because the vehicle speed and power demands vary rapidly in stop-and-go driving. The effects of this on-off engine operation on fuel usage and emissions for the parallel hybrids are neglected in most simulations at the present time, so further analysis and vehicle testing is needed to determine whether the high fuel economy and low emissions projected for parallel hybrids can be attained. The control strategies for parallel hybrids are necessarily more complex than those for series hybrids and the uncertainty in the simulation results for parallel hybrids are greater.

Applications

Toyota Prius is the most widely known example. Toyota also uses this system in the Yaris and Auris hatchbacks and Prius+ MPV hybrids, while cars from Audi, BMW, Citroen, Land Rover, Lexus, Mercedes-Benz, Peugeot, Porsche and Volkswagen work on the same basis.

When pulling away, and at speeds up to 25 kmph, the Prius only uses the electric motor for power, making it very economical for stop-start city driving. The petrol engine cuts in as speed increases, and it is used most during hard acceleration.

Advantages and disadvantages of parallel hybrid configuration

Advantages

1. Capable of attaining zero emission
2. More flexibility
3. Motor is also a generator to charge the batteries from regenerative braking or from engine power
4. Efficient design for highway applications
5. Compact system design
6. Fewer components than a series hybrid results in a more cost effective solution

Disadvantages

1. Expensive
2. Complex control
3. Requirement of proper algorithms
4. Need of high voltage to ensure efficiency

SPLIT-POWER HYBRID

Split-hybrid provides the advantages of both the systems but is more costly and complicated. In split-power hybrid, the following modes of operation are possible.

1. The transmission (planetary gear system) splits some of the power from engine to be transferred directly to the drive whereas the other part is converted into electrical energy by means of an alternator and stored in the high-voltage (HV) battery.
2. Both the electric motor and the internal combustion engine can also provide their power simultaneously for propelling the vehicle.
3. It is also possible to use electricity only.

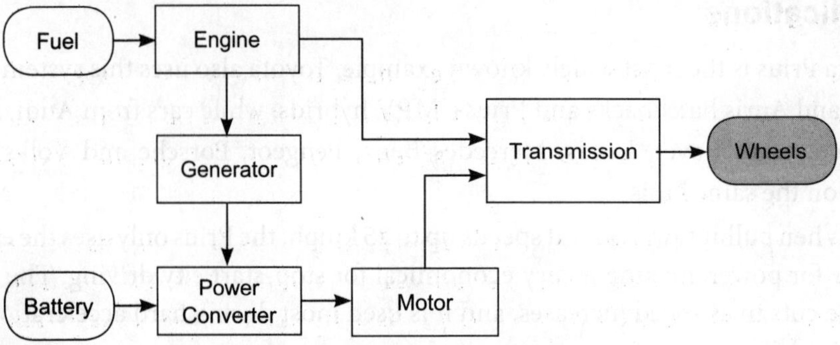

Fig. 16.3: Split-Power Hybrid

Control strategies for split power hybrid vehicles

The control strategies for dual mode hybrid vehicles are a combination of those used for series and parallel hybrids. There are so many possible hardware arrangements and associated control strategies, it is not possible to summarise them in a simple manner as was the case for series and parallel hybrids.

The objective of the dual mode operation is to use the possibility of battery charging simultaneously with the use of the engine and electric motor to power the vehicle as a means of maintaining engine operation at high efficiency at all times. At highway speeds, the engine can be used directly to power the vehicle with the engine operating at high efficiency. This mode of operation is essentially that of a parallel hybrid. At low vehicle speeds, when the battery does not need charging (state-of-charge greater than a specified value), the driveline would operate in an electric-only mode if the electric motor can provide the power required by the vehicle. If the power demand is greater than that available from the electric motor, the engine is turned on to assist the electric motor. At low speeds when the battery requires charging, the engine output is split between powering the generator and the vehicle. The possibility of splitting the engine output in this way at low vehicle speeds is the distinguishing feature of the dual mode hybrid configuration. This permits the engine to be operated near its maximum efficiency at all times and the battery to be recharged, when needed, regardless of the vehicle speed and power demand. The dual mode arrangement also reduces the need for on-off engine operation as required in the series and parallel control strategies. Dual mode hybrids are operated with the battery state-of-charge maintained in a narrow range (charge sustaining) and thus require no recharging of the battery from the wall-plug.

Application

Mistubishi Outlander, Toyota Prius and Volvo V60

Advantages and disadvantages of Split-hybrid configuration

Advantages

1. Combines the advantages of a series and a parallel configurations
2. Has a direct mechanical path for the internal combustion engine, which is very efficient in steady operating conditions like cruising.
3. Has an electromechanical path which allows for efficient operation of the IC engine in unsteady driving, such as speed variations seen in city driving.

Disadvantages

1. Further complexity and cost.

REVIEW QUESTIONS

1. What do you understand by series hybrid?
2. Give the applications of series hybrid.
3. Explain the control strategies for series hybrid vehicles.
4. Mention the advantages and disadvantages of series hybrid configuration.
5. What is meant by parallel hybrid?
6. Give the applications of parallel hybrid.
7. Explain the control strategies for parallel hybrid vehicles.
8. Mention the advantages and disadvantages of parallel hybrid configuration.
9. What is split- hybrid?
10. Mention the applications of split- hybrid.
11. Explain the control strategies for split- hybrid vehicles.
12. Mention the advantages and disadvantages of split- hybrid configuration.

17 PERFORMANCE OF HYBRID VEHICLES

UNIT OUTCOMES

Upon successful completion of this module, the student will be able to:

1. Study the requirements of EVs energy sources
2. Study the sources of electricity for EVs.
3. Identify the major types of batteries for EVs
4. Get exposed to parameters that affect the performance of a battery.
5. Identify the alternative energy storage devices.

HEVs have higher fuel economy and lower emissions than conventional engine-powered vehicles. All the vehicle types (electric, hybrid, and conventional) can be designed to have the same acceleration performance and top speed by the proper selection of the driveline components.

Acceleration and top speed

Acceleration times of 0–96 km/hr (60 mph) in less than 8 sec and top speeds in excess of 120 km/hr for passenger cars have been demonstrated for hybrid vehicles.

Fuel economy

For both the midsize and compact cars, fuel economy depends significantly on the technology used in the driveline. The use of diesel engines results in the highest fuel economy.

For the same type of engine, the fuel economy can be 10 to 20 percent higher using ultracapacitors in place of batteries as the energy storage device. The highest fuel economics are projected for vehicles using fuel cells. The fuel economies (gasoline equivalent) of the fuel cell vehicles using compressed hydrogen are about twice those of hybrid vehicles with direct injected gasoline engines and about 80 percent higher than vehicles with diesel engines. All the fuel cell vehicle designs utilised a fuel cell load-leveled with a nickel metal hydride battery permitting it to operate at high efficiency at all times.

In comparisons between the fuel economies of conventional passenger cars and those using series hybrid drivelines, the hybrid vehicles have the same weight and road load as the conventional cars. Still, the utilisation of the hybrid driveline resulted in improvement in fuel economy.

The fuel economy of series and parallel hybrid vehicles are compared for both the compact, lightweight, and midsize cars. The series hybrids are assumed to operate only in the charge sustaining mode (no battery recharging from the wall plug), but the parallel hybrids can operate in either the charge sustaining or charge depleting mode. In the case of the parallel hybrid in the charge depleting mode, the fuel economy is given for gasoline alone and at the powerplant including energy needed to recharge the batteries from the wall plug. For hybrid vehicles using gasoline engines (port injected), the fuel economy of the parallel hybrid vehicles in the charge sustaining mode (batteries charged from the engine-not from the wall plug) is 9 to 12 percent higher than that of the series hybrids. For the powerplant efficiency (33%) assumed in the calculations, the parallel hybrids operating in the charge depleting mode (battery charged only from the wall plug) had only 1 to 4 percent higher equivalent fuel economy than the same vehicle operating in the charge sustaining mode. If the batteries are recharged using electricity from a higher efficiency power plant, the fuel economy advantage of the parallel hybrid in the charge depleting mode would be lighter.

Emissions

PEVs can have significant emissions benefits over conventional vehicles. Vehicle emissions can be divided into two general categories: air pollutants, which contribute to smog, haze, and health problems; and greenhouse gases (GHGs), such as carbon dioxide and methane, which contribute to climate change. Both categories of emissions can be evaluated on a direct basis and on a life cycle basis. Direct emissions are emitted through the tailpipe, as well as through evaporation from the vehicle's fuel system and during the fueling process. EVs produce zero direct emissions. PHEVs produce zero tailpipe emissions when they are in all-electric mode, but they do produce evaporative emissions. And when using the IC engine, PHEVs do produce tailpipe emissions. However, their direct emissions are typically lower than those of comparable conventional vehicles.

Refueling

The primary advantage of the hybrid vehicle compared to the electric vehicle is that its range and refueling time can be the same or better than the conventional vehicle because it is refueled in the same manner at the fuel pump.

Regenerative braking

Electricity is generated on board the hybrid vehicles by coupling the engines to a generator or by utilising fuel cell fueled using compressed hydrogen. In all cases, electrical energy is recovered into the energy storage unit during braking using the traction motor as a generator.

REVIEW QUESTIONS

1. Are Electric vehicles (EVs) better for the environment than Internal Combustion Engine (ICE) vehicles?
2. What is the impact of battery manufacturing and production on the environment?
3. What materials is an average EV Lithium-Ion Battery composed of?
4. What is the average lifetime of a lithium-ion EV battery?
5. Can lithium and other materials contained in the EV batteries be recycled?
6. Do I need to fully charge my EV battery every day?
7. How is range affected by extreme ambient temperatures?
8. How do we make batteries less expensive?
9. How can we make batteries that store more energy?
10. How can we make batteries safer?
11. Are batteries enough for a renewable grid?
12. Which battery is best for electric vehicle?
13. What is a valid issue with electric vehicle batteries?
14. Do batteries have electrical energy?
15. How long will a lithium battery last if not charged?
16. What's the Lifespan of an Electric Car Battery?

18 FUEL CELL ELECTRIC VEHICLE (FCEV)

UNIT OUTCOMES

Upon successful completion of this module, the student will be able to:

1. Implement fuel cell in EVs.
2. Identify the different types of fuel cells for EVs.
3. Explain the components of a HFCV.

The feasible alternatives to batteries for electric vehicles and hybrid electric vehicles are fuel cells and flywheels.

Fuel cell

A fuel cell is an electrochemical energy conversion device. A fuel cell converts the chemicals hydrogen and oxygen into water and in the process it produces electricity (DC voltage) with water and heat as its by-product. In principle, a fuel cell operates like a battery. Unlike battery, a fuel cell does not run down or require recharging. It will produce electricity as long as fuel is supplied.

There are different types of fuel cells, each using a different chemistry. Fuel cells are usually classified by the type of electrolyte they use.

- Alkaline fuel cell
- Phosphoric fuel cell
- Solid oxide fuel cell
- Molten carbonate fuel cell

Construction

A fuel cell consists of two electrodes sandwiched around an electrolyte. Oxygen passes over one electrode and hydrogen over the other, generating electricity, water and heat.

The pressurized hydrogen gas (H_2) entering the fuel cell on the anode side, which is negative post of the fuel cell. It conducts the electrons that are free from the hydrogen molecules so that they can be used in an external circuit. It has channels etched into it that disperse the hydrogen gas equally over the surface of the catalyst.

Oxygen (or air) enters through the cathode, which is the positive post of fuel cell. The cathode also has channels etched into it that distribute the oxygen to the surface of the catalyst. It also conducts the electrr ns back from the external circuit to the catalyst where they can combine with the hydrogen ions and oxygen to form water.

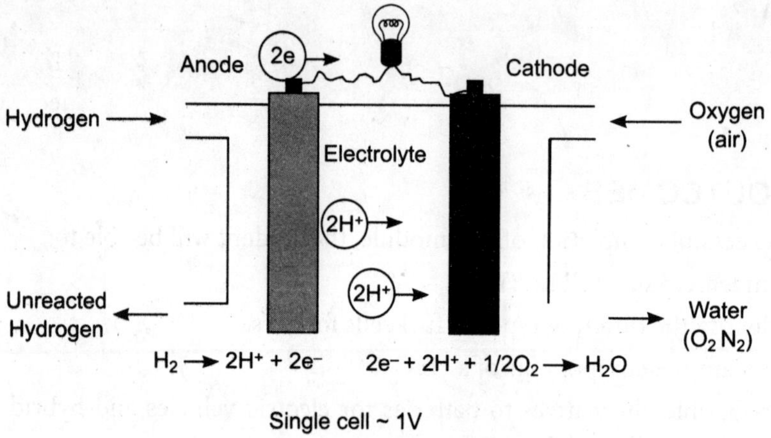

Fig. 18.1: Fuel cell

The electrolyte is the proton exchange membrane. This specially treated material only conducts positively charged ions. The membrane blocks electrons.

The catalyst is a special material that facilitates the reaction of oxygen and hydrogen. It is usually made of platinum powder very thinly coated onto carbon paper or cloth. The catalyst is rough and porous so that the maximum surface area of the platinum can be exposed to the hydrogen or oxygen. The platinum-coated side of the catalyst faces the Polymer Electrolyte Membrane (PEM).

Working principle

The pressurized hydrogen gas (H_2) entering the fuel cell on the anode side. This gas is forced through the catalyst by the pressure. When a hydrogen molecule comes in contact with the platinum on the catalyst, it splits into two H^+ ions and two electrons (e). The electrons are conducted through the anode, where they make their way through the external circuit (doing useful work such as turning a motor) and return to the cathode side of the fuel cell.

Anode side : $2H_2 \rightarrow 4H^+ + 4e^-$

Cathode side : $O_2 + 4H^+ + 4e^- \rightarrow 2H_2O$

Net reaction : $2H_2 + O_2 \rightarrow 2H_2O$

Meanwhile, on the cathode side of the fuel cell, oxygen gas (O_2) is being forced through the catalyst, where it forms two oxygen atoms. Each of these atoms has a strong negative charge. This negative charge attracts the two H^+ ions through the membrane, where they combine with an oxygen atom and two of the electrons from the external circuit to form water.

This reaction in a single fuel cell produces only about 0.7 Volts. To get this voltage up to a reasonable level, many separate fuel cells must be combined to form a fuel-cell stack.

Advantages

1. There are no emissions from the vehicle
2. Noise levels are very low
3. Vehicle is vibration free
4. Operating range is comparable to conventional vehicles
5. Highly efficient

Disadvantages

1. Storage and handling with some primary fuels such as hydrogen and natural gas is difficult
2. It is difficult to match the electrical output to fluctuating vehicle demand
3. Complicated controls are needed

FUEL CELL ELECTRIC VEHICLES (FCEVs)

Hydrogen fuel cell vehicles carry the hydrogen in special high pressure tanks, another ingredient for the power generating process is oxygen, which it acquires from the air sucked in from the environment. Electricity generated from the fuel cells goes to an electric motor which drives the wheels. Excess energy is stored in storage systems like batteries or super capacitors. FCEVs only produce water as a by product of its power generating process which is ejected out of the car through the tailpipe. The configuration of a FCEV is shown in Fig. 18.2

An advantage of such vehicles is they can produce their own electricity which emits no carbon, enabling it to reduce its carbon footprint further than any other EV. Another major advantage of these are, and maybe the most important one right now, refilling these vehicles takes the same amount of time required to fill a conventional vehicle at a fuel station. This makes adoption of these vehicles more likely in the near future.

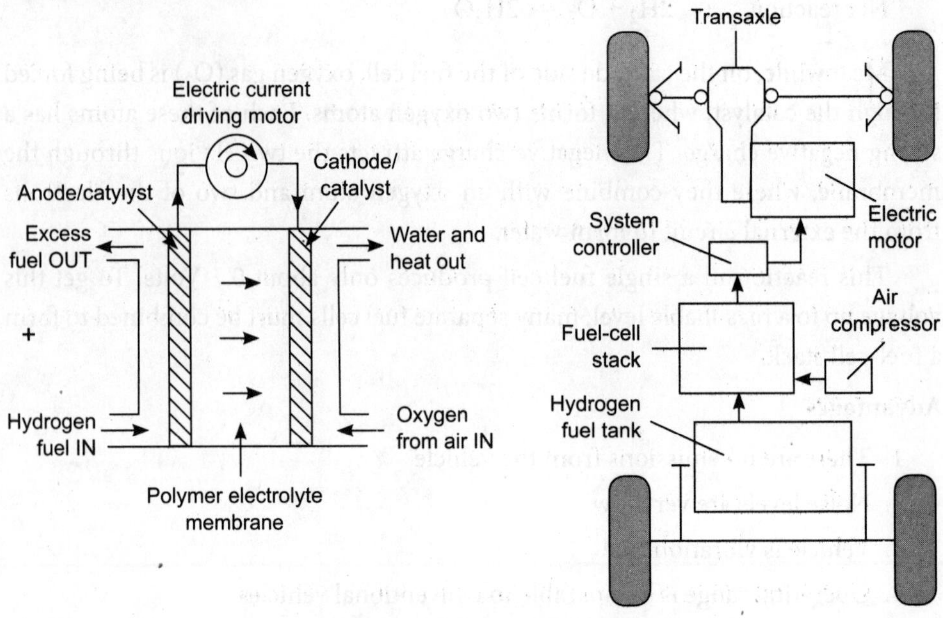

Fig. 18.1: Configuration of a FCEV.

A major current obstacle in adopting this technology is the scarcity of hydrogen fuel stations. Another disadvantage is the high cost of fuel cells that cost more than ₹ 12000 per kW, which is far greater than IC engine (less than ₹ 3000 per kW). There are also concerns regarding safety in case of flammable hydrogen leaking out of the tanks. If these obstacles were eliminated, FCEVs could really represent the future of cars.

Components of a Hydrogen Fuel Cell Electric Car

Battery (auxiliary)

In an electric drive vehicle, the auxiliary battery provides electricity to start the car before the traction battery is engaged and also powers vehicle accessories.

Battery pack

This battery stores energy generated from regenerative braking and provides supplemental power to the electric traction motor.

DC/DC converter

This device converts higher-voltage DC power from the traction battery pack to the lower-voltage DC power needed to run vehicle accessories and recharge the auxiliary battery.

Electric traction motor

Using power from the fuel cell and the traction battery pack, this motor drives the vehicle's wheels. Some vehicles use motor generators that perform both the drive and regeneration functions.

Fuel cell stack

An assembly of individual membrane electrodes that use hydrogen and oxygen to produce electricity.

Fuel filler

This is a filler or "nozzle" used to add fuel to the tank.

Fuel tank (hydrogen)

Stores hydrogen gas on board the vehicle until it's needed by the fuel cell.

Power electronics controller

This unit manages the flow of electrical energy delivered by the fuel cell and the traction battery, controlling the speed of the electric traction motor and the torque it produces.

Thermal system (cooling)

This system maintains a proper operating temperature range of the fuel cell, electric motor, power electronics, and other components.

Transmission (electric)

The transmission transfers mechanical power from the electric traction motor to drive the wheels.

Advantages and Disadvantages of FCEV

Advantages

- Very low emission
- High efficiency

- Not dependent on supply of electricity
- High price
- Available commercially
- Better driving range

Disadvantages

- Cost of fuel cell
- Lack of hydrogen refueling infrastructure
- Feasible way to produce fuel

Applications

Toyota Mirai and Honda Clarity.

REVIEW QUESTIONS

1. What is fuel cell?
2. How do you classify the fuel cell by the type of electrolyte?
3. List out the different types of fuel cell.
4. Explain the working principle of fuel cell.
5. Mention the advantages and disadvantages of fuel cell.
6. Briefly explain the components of hydrogen FCEVs.
7. Give the advantages and disadvantages of FCEVs.
8. Mention the applications of FCEVs.

19 COMPARISON

UNIT OUTCOMES

Upon successful completion of this module, the student will be able to:

1. Compare the EVs with that of ICEVs.
2. Compare the BEV, PHEV, FCEV and ICEV.

A Comparison between EVs and standard Internal Combustion Engine Vehicles (ICEVs)

Internal Combustion Engine Vehicle (ICEV)

- **More bang:** Petrochemicals are controlled explosions that deliver a large force for a small amount of fuel and subsequently less weight in comparison to current batteries. There is less inertia to overcome when accelerating.
- **Wasted energy:** There is no way to apply the vehicle's latent momentum back into a force that can be reutilised to further accelerate without adding significant weight to the vehicle defeating the advantages of that regeneration.
- **Mass distribution and wasted weight:** Two large mass centres: the fuel tank and engine. A heavy drive train and chassis are required to support these mass structures.
- **Air pollution:** ICEVs exhaust a mixture of gases and ions that cause harm to the environment and in sufficient concentrations harm to humans directly.
- **Refuelling:** Refuelling can be achieved quickly.
- **Hazardous chemical risk:** Petrol stations are an environmental risk and a safety hazard requiring bulk storage of explosive toxic fuels.
- **Range:** Petrol fuelled vehicles have a range of 400–600 km

Battery Electric Vehicle (BEV)

- **Mass distribution:** Wheels can be driven directly with a motor at each wheel or the wheel can be the motor. The advantages of smaller masses at motor locations, where maximum force is required, allow for more freedom of design, lower centres of gravity and better handling opportunities. Flexibility in weight distribution also allows for more safety features to be built into the overall design.
- **Energy conservation:** Power can be regenerated using the vehicle's latent momentum during braking.
- **Refuelling depots:** Refuelling depots can be set up almost anywhere at low cost and can be easily utilised without the need for monitoring.
- **Induction recharging:** Vehicles can simply be parked over induction pads or even recharged on the move. No hazardous chemical storage required.
- **Car mass:** Most of the weight will be in the battery with better more efficient batteries currently being developed.
- **More space in the interior:** Without the two large masses (fuel tank and engine) present in ICEVs, different designs can be constructed to utilise the space more effectively.
- **Solar paneling:** If stranded in remote areas, solar panels mounted in the car body allow for the vehicle to be recharged.
- **Vehicle emissions:** There are no gas emissions and low noise emissions in a BEV.
- **Range:** BEVs can have a range of 450 km.
- **Fast charge:** currently 1 hour for 450 km of range but with minimal development could be equivalent to that of petrol vehicles.

Table 19.1: Comparison of ICE vehicles and Battery EVs

Parameters	ICE Vehicles	EV Vehicles
Power source	IC Engine	Motor (+Engine)
Specific energy	High for fuel	Low for battery
Power density	High	Low
Range	> 480 kms / fill	< 160 kms / charge
Efficiency	Engine efficiency ~45%	Motor efficiency ~ 80%
Max. torque	Need to pick up some speed to deliver max. torque	Produce max. torque instantly after starting of motor
Gear system	Needs complex gear system	Needs only one gear system

Parameters	ICE Vehicles	EV Vehicles
Noise	Noisy operation	Quiet operation
Infrastructure	Ample refilling infrastructure	Lacks charging infrastructure
Refilling/Charging time	Short (< minutes)	Long (0.5 to 8 hours)
Fuel	Uses only hydrocarbons	Uses electricity from many resources
Running cost	High	Low
Maintenance cost	High	Low
Emissions	Emits harmful gases like HC, CO, NOx, etc.	No tailpipe emissions
Space occupied	Fuel tank takes less space	Battery takes large space
Weight	Less fuel weight	Batteries are very heavy
Energy recovered	Braking energy not recovered	Braking energy recovered

The table 19.2 is referring to the comparison of BEV, PHEV, FCEV and ICE types of vehicles, where the main concerns cover the costs, range, speed, fuel economy, emissions, etc. and the quantitative differences between them.

Table 19.2: Comparison of BEV, PHEV, FCEV and ICEV

	Internal Combustion Engines Vehicles (ICEVs)	Battery Electric Vehicles (BEVs)	Hybrid Electric Vehicles (HEVs)	Fuel Cell Electric vehicles (FCEVs)
Reference	Volkswagon Golf 1.4TSI	Nissan Leaf	Toyota Prius III	Honda FCX Clarity
Prime mover	ICE	Battery, Electric motor	ICE, Electric motor	PEM fuel cells and Electric motor
Fuel	Petrol, diesel and alternative fuel	Electricity	Petrol or diesel as main fuel	Hydrogen
Top speed, km/h	200	150	180	160
Acceleration, s	9.5	7	10.4	10
Range, km	888	118-175	1152	386
Running cost per km, Rs	9	0.8	6	3
Fuel economy, kmpl or kmpl equivalent	19	31	42	34
Tailpipe emissions	Higher	0	Lower	0

REVIEW QUESTIONS

1. Compare the internal combustion engine vehicle with battery electric vehicle.
2. Give the comparison of battery electric vehicle, plug-in hybrid electric vehicle, fuel cell electric vehicle and internal combustion electric vehicle.

20 TRANSMISSION IN EVs

UNIT OUTCOMES

Upon successful completion of this module, the student will be able to:

1. Differentiate transmission system used in EVs & HEVs from Conventional transmission system.
2. Identify the transmission systems used in EVs & HEVs

SINGLE-SPEED TRANSMISSION

Most of the Electric cars are single-speed transmission vehicles. Speed-torque characteristic of electric machines makes them most suitable for traction. The ability to meet high torque demands at low speed is the reason why a multispeed gearbox is unnecessary in an electric car.

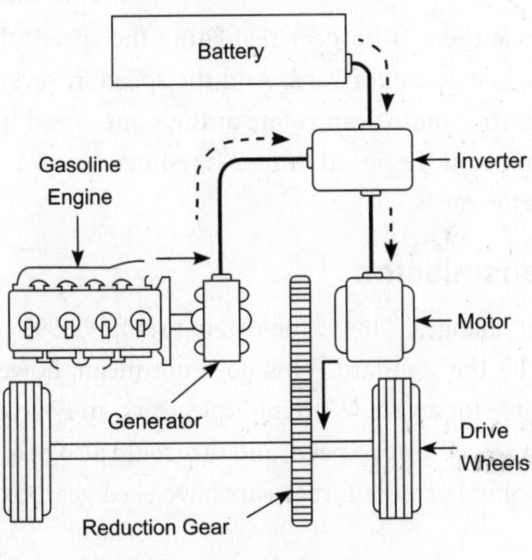

Fig. 20.1: Single speed transmission

One of the biggest differences in the majority of EVs, when compared to conventional vehicles is the absence of a gear shifter, simply because they have just one gear. A diesel or petrol powered car's internal combustion engine develops its power and torque at different RPM's (revolutions per minute) and therefore it needs a gearbox with various gear ratios to effectively transfer the power to the driven wheels and keep the engine in its "happy power band".

EVs generally have very compact drive selectors. After starting the motor, all the driver needs to do is push a button or turn a dial to select "D" to move forward , "R" to reverse and "P" to park. Some people may feel this is similar to what you do in a regular car with an automatic transmission or gearbox, but it's not. Automatic transmissions have multiple gears or speeds that are selected and shifted automatically as per the pressure on the accelerator or brake pedal. But most EVs only have one gear, which means no gear shifts, either manual or automatic. And as it has only one gear, it's also not possible to stall an EV.

And as there is just one gear regulating the electric motor, it means that EVs don't even have a reverse gear. This is because an electric motor can turn clockwise or anti-clockwise and the direction in which it's rotating, determines if the car will move forward, or back. And reversing the direction, in which the motor is rotating, can be done by just giving an electrical input via the drive selector switch or knob. In a conventional car, the gear selector is a mechanical device to aid shifting of gears. But in an EV, the electric motor is controlled or regulated by an advanced motor controller unit that gets inputs from the electric drive selector. This drive selector is like a smart input device that does not do anything mechanical, but instead electrically instructs the motor which way it needs to turn.

Interestingly, since there is no gear regulating the speed, the acceleration in reverse is as fast as while going forward. And the speed in reverse is only limited by software as the electric motor can rotate at the same speed in either direction. Fascinatingly, this means, if the speed limiter is removed, an EV can go just as fast backwards as it does forwards.

Multi-speed Transmission

Single speed, no gear changes. This is the driving setup 99.99% of electric vehicle drivers are used to. It's the standard. This does not mean, however, that a multi-ratio setup isn't possible for an EV. With multiple gears, an EV could achieve better low-end acceleration as well as top speed, and this could also help increase its range marginally. In fact, some Formula E race cars have used gearboxes with up to five speeds, while the Porsche Taycan employs a two-speed gearbox. The two-speed transmission is only arriving now partly because it's complicated. Multispeed transmissions must be robust to deal with the massive amounts of torque that electric motors can generate in a very short period of time.

However, given that a single ratio provides the bulk of the required performance, nearly every EV today uses a single-speed unit rather than have to manage the complexity of a multi-ratio gearbox as well as the added cost – the last thing an EV needs. And this is why EVs today have no gearbox, or rather, just a single speed unit.

REVIEW QUESTIONS

1. Classify the transmission systems used in EVs.
2. Brief about single-speed transmission.
3. List out the merits of single-speed transmission.
4. Give the importance of multi-speed transmission in EVs and HEVs.

21 HYBRID CARS IN INDIA

UNIT OUTCOMES

Upon successful completion of this module, the student will be able to:

1. Get exposed to HEVs in India.
2. Compare the features of different HEVs available in Indian market.

Hybrid cars have become an alternative to petrol and diesel cars. Earlier, only the environmentally-conscious consumers opted for hybrid cars. However, now that the Indian government is trying to phase out petrol and diesel cars in an effort to protect the environment from air pollution, more customers are purchasing hybrid and fully electric vehicles.

The Faster Adoption and Manufacturing of Hybrid and Electric (FAME) vehicles' scheme, introduced in 2015, offers incentives in terms of exemptions of road tax and VAT for Hybrid cars in India. Also recently the Delhi Government has reduced the VAT paid on Hybrid Cars in India from 12.5% to 5% igniting consumers' interest in the HEVs further.

The potential in the segment is huge, with much needed benefits over other types of cars which work favorably in the long term. And going by how technology is progressing, one can surely say that the future of automobiles lies in the hands of Hybrid Cars indicating a better and cleaner future.

MG Hector Hybrid

The MG Hector 1.5 L Super Hybrid is the base variant in the hybrid line-up of Hector. The 1.5 L petrol engine of the SUV is capable of producing a max power of 143 PS @ 5000rpm and max torque of 250 Nm. The engine comes mated to a 6-speed MT. There is also a 48 V mild hybrid battery for additional torque to counter the turbo lag. MG Hector 1.5 L Super Hybrid mileage in hybrid variants will be around 15.81 kmpl.

Toyota Prius

One of the first plug-in hybrid cars in India is the Toyota Prius launched in the Indian car market in 2012.

Although with greener emissions and a good fuel economy of 23.91 kmpl, the Toyota Prius comes at a hefty price range of 38.1-39.8 lakhs and available in 7 colours in India. The 5-seater car is powered by a 1798cc petrol engine that produces 97 bhp power. The engine is paired with an automatic gearbox and a CVT-speed system. The car has an infotainment system with Android Auto, Apple CarPlay, and MirrorLink. It can deliver 40 kmpl mileage.

Toyota Camry Hybrid

The next green offering from Toyota is the series hybrid car- The Toyota Camry. The Camry is entirely different from the Prius, with the Camry utilising a nickel metal hydride battery while retaining its large engine. The standard Camry is elegant and brings sophistication in its interiors making it the ideal chauffeur-driven car.

This car is powered by a 2.5-litre petrol engine and an electric motor that produces 205 PS power and 270 Nm torque. The engine is paired with a CVT system. With the Hybrid Synergy Drive, the car can be switched from the petrol mode to the electric mode easily. The other modes include EV and Eco modes. Toyota Camry Hybrid delivers 19.16 kmplmileage.
The green hybrid car in India comes at a hefty price of 30.3-33.2 lakhs, 2019.

Toyota Yaris Hybrid

This car was first launched in 2015 at the Shanghai Motor Show. The XC90 T8 Hybrid is priced at ₹1.25 crore. The car is powered by a T8 twin engine - a 2-litre turbocharged petrol engine and a 9.2 kWh Li-ion battery. The supercharged petrol engine produces 402 bhp power and 640 Nm torque. The engine is paired with an 8-speed automatic gearbox for transmission. When fully charged, the electric motors of the SUV can travel a distance of 32 km. The car can go from 0 to 100 kmph in under 5.6 seconds.

BMW i8

This electric car is powered by a 1.5-litre, 3-cylinder engine that generates 320 Nm torque and 231 PS power to the rear tyres while Li-ion batteries power the front wheels. The battery can be charged in just 4 hours. The car can go from 0 to 100 kmph in under 4.4 seconds. It delivers 47.45 kmpl mileage. The ex-showroom price of BMW i8 Hybrid is ₹2.62 crore, 2021.

BMW i3

The BMW i3 won the 2015 Green Car of the Year Award at the 2014 LA Auto Show. This car is powered by a 170 hp electric motor that produces 250 Nm torque. Courtesy of a 650cc engine, the car gives 160-300 km mileage. The car is priced at ₹1 crore.

Mahindra Scorpio S10 Intelli-Hybrid

This car is powered by a 2.2-litre Intelli-Hybrid engine that produces 120 bhp power and 280 Nm torque. The engine is paired with a 5-speed manual gearbox. The SUV is priced at ₹11.47 lakh. It seats 7 to 9 persons comfortably. The car delivers 16.36 kmpl mileage.

Mercedes C-Class C300h

This diesel/electric hybrid has a top-speed of 152 mph. It is powered by a 2.143cc engine that produces 231 bhp power and 500 Nm torque. The car can go from 0 to 62 km/h in just 6.40 seconds.

Mitsubishi Outlander PHEV

The 2017 Mitsubishi Outlander PHEV can detect blind spots and pedestrians to prevent accidents. The car comes with 3 driving modes - hybrid, electric and parallel hybrid. The new Mitsubishi Outlander is likely to be powered by a 2.0-2.4-litre engine that produces 150-180 bhp power.

Audi A3 e-tron

The Audi e-Tron Quattro have 3 electric motors, one in the front with a 95 kW battery and 2 at the back. The combined power of the electric motors is 430-496 bhp power. The expected mileage of the electric SUV is 500 km on full charge, The car is capable of going from 0 to 100 kmph in just 4.6 seconds.

Volkswagen Passat GTE Plug-In Hybrid

This car was launched in 2016. It is powered by Volkswagen's E hybrid technology. The car has a 1.4-litre TSI turbocharged petrol engine that produces 154 bhp power while the electric motor produces 113 bhp power and 400 Nm torque. The engine is paired with a 6-speed DSG gearbox. The electric motor is mated to a 9.9 kWh Li-ion battery. The car can go from 0 to 100 km/h in under 8 seconds. The driver can opt for 4 driving modes - Hybrid, GTE, Battery Charge, and E-mode.

Volvo XC90 T8 Plug-In Hybrid

This 7-seater luxury SUV is powered by a T8 twin engine plug-in hybrid electric unit. The electric motor is mated to a Li-ion battery that produces 10.4 kWh. The engine is paired with a 8-speed automatic gearbox. It gives a combined power output of 402 bhp and 640 Nm torque.

Maruti Suzuki Ertiga SHVS

This car is one of the first semi-hybrid vehicles to be introduced in the country with the Smart Hybrid Vehicle by Suzuki technology (SHVS). This car is powered by a 1.3-litre multijet diesel engine that generates 89 bhp power and 200 Nm torque. The engine is paired with a 5-speed manual gearbox. The Ertiga SHVS delivers 24.52 kmplmileage.

Maruti Suzuki Ciaz SHVS

India's largest carmaker introduced the SHVS technology first in the Ciaz model. The sedan is powered by a 1.3-litre Multijet diesel engine. The Integrated Starter Generator (ISG) helps the engine perform better and increase fuel efficiency. The Ciaz SHVS delivers 28.09 kmplmileage.

Honda Accord Hybrid

This car was launched in October 2017. The car is powered by a 2-litre, 4-cylinder petrol engine that generates 145 PS power. It has a 1.3 kWh lithium-ion battery pack that generates 215 PS power and 175 Nm torque. The engine is paired with an E-CVT system, capable of producing power from 2 motors. Honda Accord Hybrid is a fuel-efficient car with 23.1 kmpl mileage.

Honda Civic Hybrid

When the prolific Honda Civic received a Series Hybrid Car System, it became one of the first hybrid cars in India along with the Prius. Combined with the durability and reliability of Honda with the benefits of fuel efficiency of hybrid cars' system, the Civic makes for a great Hybrid Car to consider.

The Civic has now been discontinued by Honda, but a pre-owned Civic Hybrid can be bought from a Used Car Portal.

REVIEW QUESTIONS

1. What are the challenges of hybrid electric vehicles in India?
2. What are the environmental impacts of hybrid electric vehicles in India?
3. What modifications are carried out in HEVs to suit Indian roads?
4. Who makes HEVs today in India?

22 STEERING SYSTEM FOR EVs AND HEVs

UNIT OUTCOMES

Upon successful completion of this module, the student will be able to:

1. Identify the steering systems suitable for EVs and HEVs.
2. Get exposed to components of steering system used in EVs and HEVs.

EVs and HEVs typically utilise electronically controlled steering systems.

ELECTRONIC POWER STEERING

The electronically controlled power steering improves steering ability and performance. This power steering reduces the steering effort when driving at low speeds and provides a corrective action when driving at high speeds.

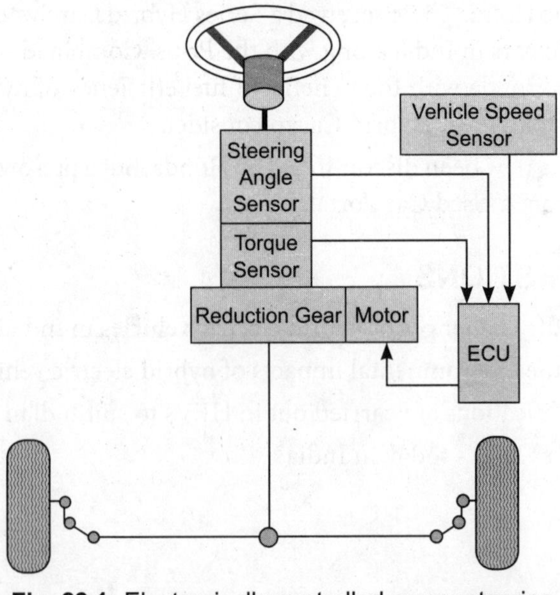

Fig. 22.1: Electronically controlled power steering

It consists of wheel speed sensor, a steering sensor (torque, angular velocity), an electronic control unit, a drive unit and a motor. Signal output from each sensor are input to ECU and necessary steering assistance is calculated and applied by the drive unit to control the operation of the motor.

(a) Power steering ECU

The power steering ECU calculates assisting power based on steering torque signals from the torque sensor and vehicle speed signals from the skid control ECU. For vehicles without ABS, the power steering ECU receives vehicle speed signals from the speedometer.

(b) Torque sensor

The torque sensor detects the steering effort generated when the steering wheel is turned and converts it to an electrical signal.

(c) EPS motor

The EPS motor is activated by the current from the power steering ECU and generates torque to assist the steering effort.

Advantages of electronic power steering

1. Reduction of driver's burden
2. Smoothness in steering operation
3. Reduction of kick back
4. Correction of steering reaction forces

STEER-BY-WIRE SYSTEM

Modern electric and hybrid electric concept cars use more advanced steering systems, such as the steer-by-wire system. There are many concept EVs and HEVs, such as the Audi A2, that use this technology in their steering system.

Steer-by-Wire systems are a further development of today's electric power steering systems. In a conventional system where the steering wheel is mechanically connected to the road, it is still possible to steer the vehicle in case of electric power assisted steering (EPAS) failure. This is due to the fact that modern power steering only functions as an assisting feature.

Steer-by-Wire system allows independent control of each wheel, and eliminates all the mechanical components of the steering system. An actuator on the steering wheel produces the necessary steering torque (feedback actuator) to create an authentic steering feel for the driver. Another actuator on the steering gear steers the road wheels (steering actuator). This arrangement provides the best maneuverability and handling performance for the vehicle.

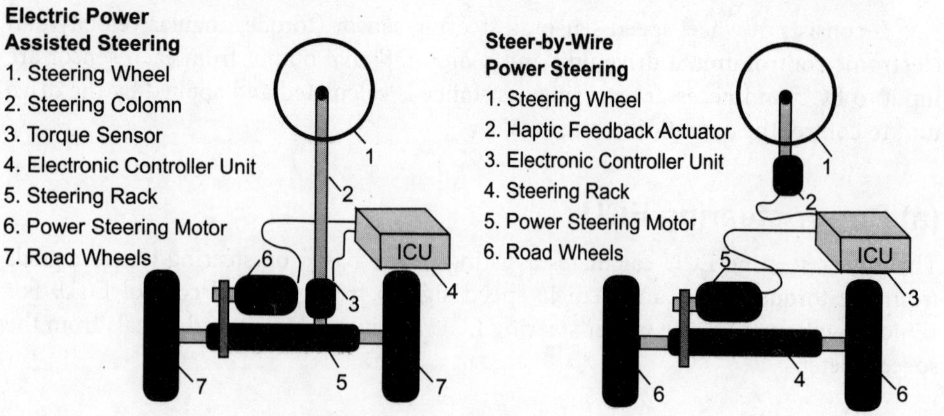

Fig. 22.2: Steer-by-wire system

REVIEW QUESTIONS

1. List the steering systems used in EVs.
2. List the steering systems used in HEVs.
3. Discuss the working of electronic power steering in EVs.
4. Briefly explain the components used in electronic power steering.
5. What are the advantages of electronic power steering in EVs.
6. What is steer-by-wire system?

23 SUSPENSION SYSTEM FOR EVs AND HEVs

UNIT OUTCOMES

Upon successful completion of this module, the student will be able to:

1. Identify the suspension systems suitable for EVs and HEVs.
2. Get exposed to components of suspension system used in EVs and HEVs.

The differences between the suspension systems of current EVs/HEVs and conventional cars are insignificant. For example, the Toyota Prius has a MacPherson suspension system in the front axle and an H-beam suspension system in the rear axle, which is the same system as conventional cars in this class. The Nissan Leaf is another example of an electric vehicle that also uses MacPherson and H-beam suspension systems in the front and rear axles, which are the dominant suspension system configurations for compact cars. The following are few types used in different models of EVs and HEVs.

MACPHERSON STRUT TYPE

This is the most widely used independent suspension system for the front suspension of small and medium sized cars.

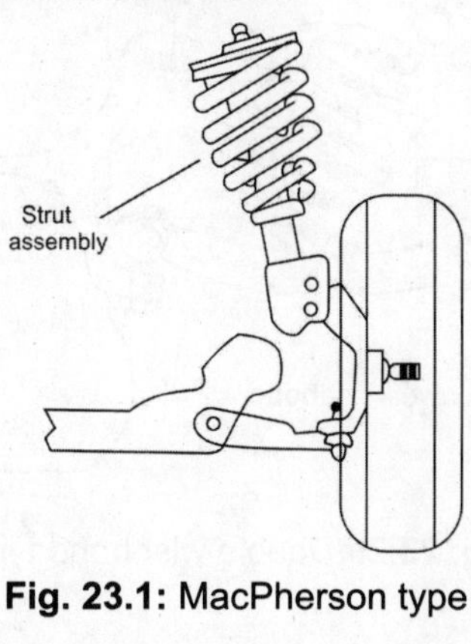

Fig. 23.1: MacPherson type

In this type only lower wishbones are used. A strut containing shock absorber and the spring carries also the stub axle on which the wheel is mounted. The wishbone is hinged to the cross member and positions the wheel as well as resists acceleration, braking and side forces.

Characteristics

- The construction of the suspension is relatively simple.
- Since there is a small number of parts, it is light, so unsprung weight can be reduced.
- Since the space taken up by the suspension is small, the usable space in the engine compartment can be increased.
- Since the distance between suspension support points is great, there is little disturbance of the front wheel alignment due to installation error or part manufacturing error. Therefore, except for toe-in, alignment adjustments are ordinarily unnecessary.

Applications

Front suspension of Hyundai Kona Electric, Mahindra e2o NXT, Mahindra E Verito, Tata Nexon EV, Tata eMO ev, etc.

DOUBLE WISHBONE

Double wishbone type is used widely for the front and rear suspensions of passenger cars. This type is also referred to as short-and-long arm (SLA) suspension. It consists of upper and lower wishbone arms pivoted to the frame members. The vehicle weight is transmitted from the body and cross-member to the coil spring through which it goes to the lower wishbone member.

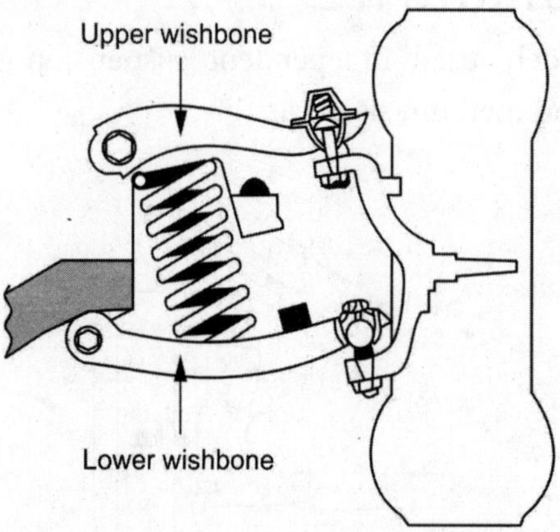

Fig. 23.2: Double wishbone type

The wishbone arms are like the chicken wishbone or letter V in shape, because of which the system is so called. Because of this V-shape, the wishbones not only position the wheels and transmit the vehicle load to the springs, but these also resist acceleration, braking and cornering (side) forces. The upper arms are shorter in length than the lower ones. This helps to keep tyre remains in a more constant position, thus minimising tyre wear. The wishbone type is the most popular independent suspension system.

Characteristics

In this type, the upper control arm is shorter than the lower control arm. During wheel jounce and rebound travel, the upper control arm moves in a shorter arc than the lower arm. This action moves the top of the tyre in and out slightly, but the bottom of the tyre remains in a more constant position.

Applications

Jaguar I-Pace, Tesla model X.

SEMI-TRAILING ARM TYPE

This type is used for the rear suspension in a few models.

Characteristics

With this suspension, the amount by which the toe angle and camber change (due to the up-and-down motion of the wheels) can be controlled by varying the length of each arm and setting the arm installation angle and angle of axis sway at the design stage, in order to determine the handling characteristics of the car.

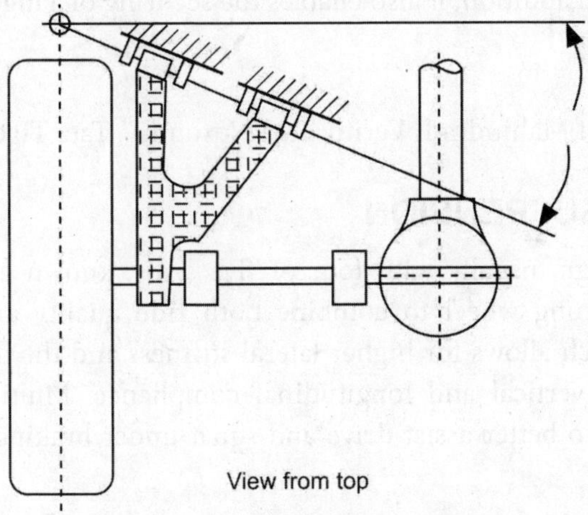

Fig. 23.3 Semi-trailing arm type

Applications

Tata eMo ev

TRAILING ARM WITH TWIST-BEAM TYPE

This type is mainly used in the rear suspension of compact front-engine front-wheel drive (FF) vehicles and employs a structure consisting of a suspension arm and stabilizer bar (torsion bar) welded to a twistable axle beam.

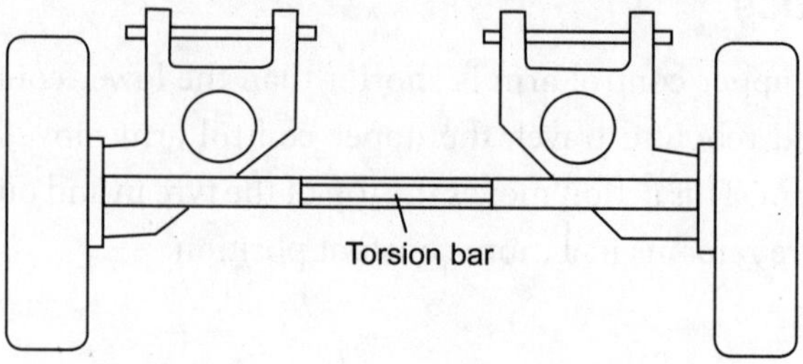

Fig. 23.4: Trailing arm with twist beam type

When the wheels bound and rebound in opposite directions, the twisting movement of the ends of the suspension arms is translated into a twisting of the rear axle beam, built-in stabilizer and rear suspension arms. The twisting of the rear axle beam and stabilizer generates a reactive force which opposes the twisting of the suspension arms, aiding the coil springs in providing roll rigidity to minimize body rolling, thus yielding greater steering stability, thereby maintaining vehicle stability.

Due to its simple structure and compact size, unsprung weight can be reduced for a better ride. In addition, it also enables the securing of a luggage space.

Applications

Rear suspension of Mahindra E Verito, Tata Nexon EV, Tata Tigor EV XE, etc.

MULTI-LINK SUSPENSION

A multi-link design, usually with four or five arms, known as links, allows an independently-sprung wheel to combine both ride quality and handling. The multi-link approach allows for higher lateral stiffness and the desired toe change with appropriate vertical and longitudinal compliance. Multi-link setups can also be designed to better assist drive and squat under braking and acceleration respectively.

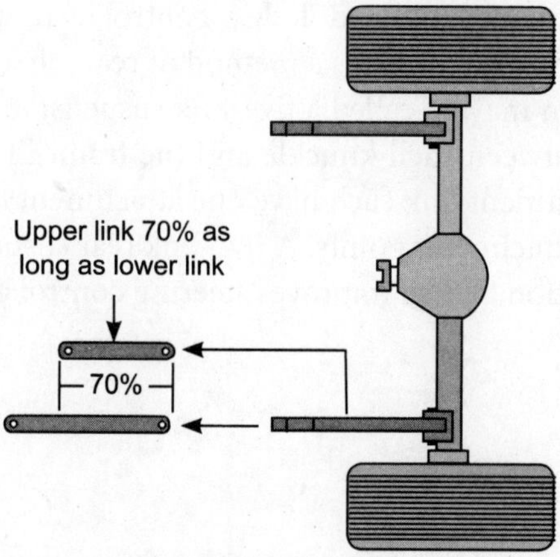

Fig. 23.5: Four-link suspension

Four-link type

This type is used for the rear suspension. It provides the best riding comfort of all the rigid-axle suspensions.

Characteristics

- Since axle positioning is accomplished by a linkage, soft springs can be used and riding comfort is good.
- Due to the geometrical layout of the linkages, nose diving during braking and rear-end squat during acceleration are prevented. Also the up-and-down movement of the front end of the differential during bounding and rebounding can be minimized by making the upper control arms shorter than the lower control arms. This in turn means that the floor over the nose of the differential can be lowered, allowing more passenger compartment space.
- Use of coil springs minimizes friction in the suspension, so minute shocks from the road surface can be absorbed and riding comfort can be improved.
- Generally, when this suspension system is used in the rear, the linkage is located forward of the axle, and as a result, the capacity of the trunk can be larger on passenger cars.

Five-link type

A trailing arm is connected from the lower end of the knuckle to the frame. Large insulating bushings are mounted at each trailing arm attachment location. The trailing arm prevents fore-and-aft wheel movement. An adjustment link is also connected from the lower end of the knuckle to the frame through insulating bushings. The adjustment link and lower control arm prevent lateral wheel movement and this link also provides a method of rear wheel toe adjustment. This type of rear suspension may be called a five-link suspension because there are five attachments points between each knuckle and the frame. The lower control arm, trailing arm and adjustment link each have one attachment location and the upper control arm has two attachment points. A five-link rear suspension provides a very stable rear wheel position, which improves steering control and rear tyre tread life.

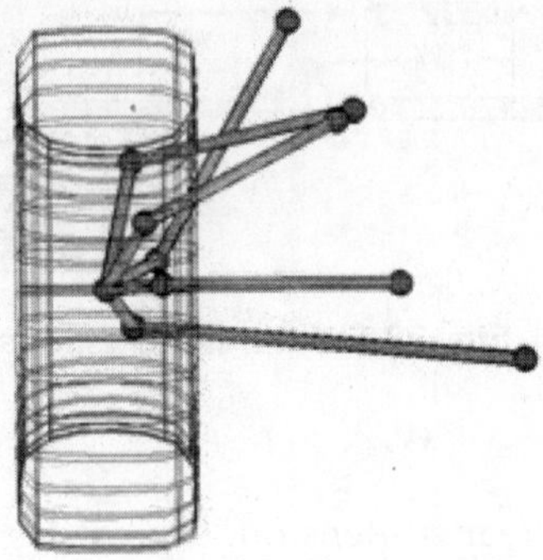

Fig. 23.6: Five-link suspension

In the other design, there are two non-parallel unequal length trailing links per side to give longitudinal location of the axle. Parallel links of equal length would give the closest approach to vertical motion of the axle under bounce and rebound, but the links are usually given a convergence on an effective pivot centre, thus giving a measure of anti-dive effect. The fifth link is required to give lateral location. A panhard rod does not give perfect location but is a simple solution. The rod should be as long as possible to constrain the axle to move in a "flat arc". One end of the rod is attached to a bracket on the body/frame, the other to a bracket on the axle casing on the opposite side. Rubber bushes are used on all five links to reduce the transmission of vibrations to the body.

Applications

Rear suspension of Hyundai Kona Electric

AIR SUSPENSION

Air suspension is a type of vehicle suspension powered by an engine driven or electric air pump or compressor. This pump pressurises the air, using compressed air as a spring. Air suspension replaces conventional steel springs. If the engine is left off for an extended period, the car will settle to the ground. The purpose of air suspension is to provide a smooth ride quality and in some cases self-leveling.

Operation

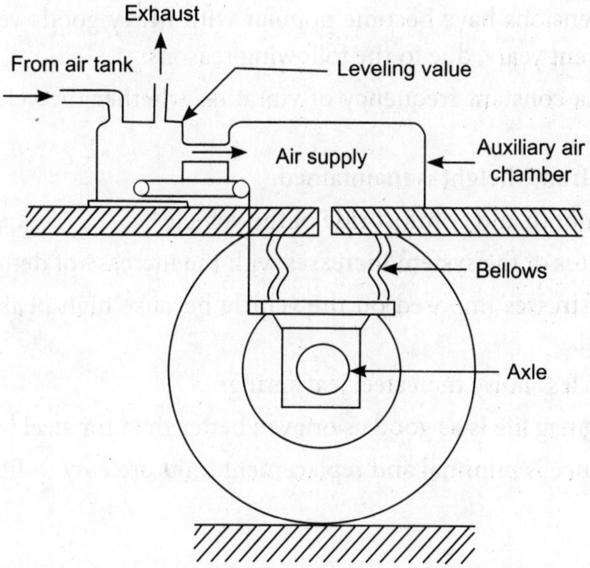

Fig. 23.7: Air suspension

The air suspension comprises a compressor supplying air to an air tank, a leveling valve to maintain a pressure a fixed distance between the chassis frame and ground and four air bags (rubber bellows). Each air bag is filled with compressed air and supports the weight of the vehicle. The air bag is placed between the chassis frame and the axle beam. As the load is applied to the frame, the air bags get compressed, actuating the leveling valves (control actuators). Air from the tank fills the compressed air bags and hence raises the level of the frame. The supply of air is automatically cut as soon as the frame reaches a predetermined level. The air from the air bag gets released as soon as the load on the chassis frames decreases. The leveling valve again does this.

Air pressure is supplied to the air-bags from the air braking system which may be as high as 8 bar, but the supply pressure is reduced before it is introduced to the air-bag to around 5 bar when the vehicle is fully laden and decreasing to about 2.5 bar in the unladen state. Rolling-lobe air bags can operate at bounce frequencies as low as 80 cycles per minute fully laden, rising to roughly 100 cycles per minute when unladen.

Tesla's smart air suspention features sensor calibrated air suspension coupled with programming that can adjust the suspension's height based on GPS location, speed and driving conditions.

Advantages

Air spring suspensions have become popular with heavy goods vehicles, coaches and buses in recent years, due to the following reasons:

- Maintain a constant frequency of vibration whether the vehicle is laden or unladen.
- Constant frame height is maintained.
- It gives smooth and comfort ride of the vehicle.
- The stiffness of the system increases with the increase of deflection.
- It lowers stresses imposed on the vehicle because high peak axle loads are eliminated.
- Generates less noise than steel leaf springs
- Air spring bag life is as good as or even better than for steel leaf springs.
- Maintenance is minimal and replacement units are easy to fit.

Application

Tesla models and continental

REGENERATIVE SUSPENSION SYSTEM

Fig. 23.8: Regenerative suspension layout

The regenerative shock absorber (GenShock) works on energy recovery through the use of an active damper. The technology is contained in a device mounted to the outside of each shock that regulates the flow of oil through the shock absorber. The device houses its own control unit, an electric motor and an electro-hydraulic gear pump, and controls the flow of fluid in the shocks to adjust the damping rate. The process is reversed when the shock is regenerating energy.

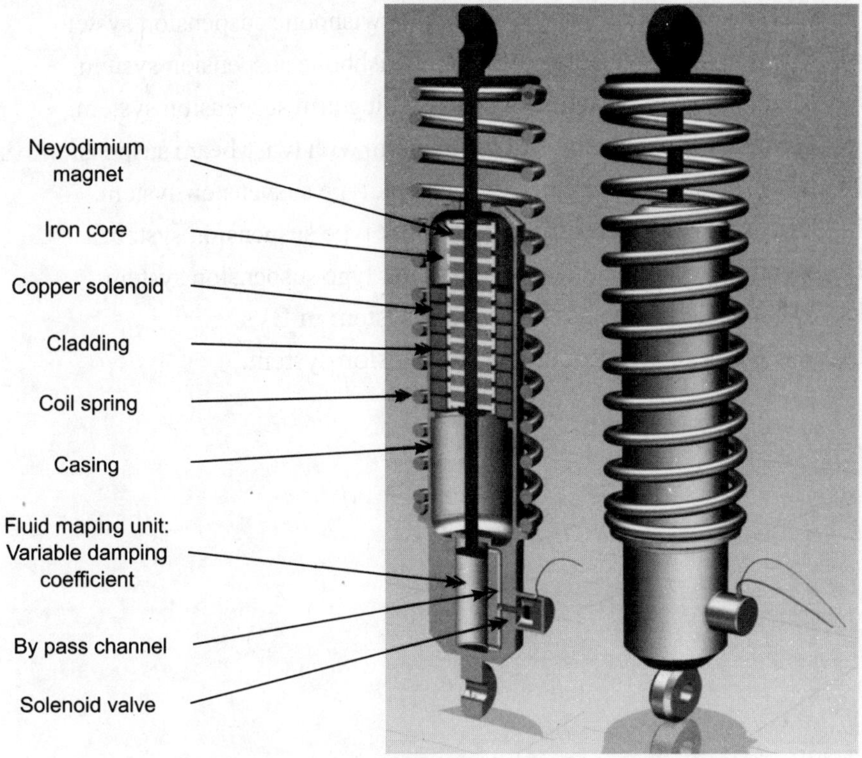

Fig. 23.9: Regenerative shock absorber

With the weight of the Tesla Model S exceeding 2000 kg, there's potential to convert enough kinetic energy, as the vehicle experiences lateral forces through cornering, during acceleration and while braking. The movement of the piston within the shock absorber pushes fluid past the GenShock's electro-hydraulic gear pump, which drives the electric motor and converts the kinetic energy into electricity that is ultimately fed back into the power supply. This captured energy would be used to propel the vehicle, and this would conceivably increase EV car ranges.

Naturally the regenerative characteristics are most realised when travelling through poor-quality roads.

REVIEW QUESTIONS

1. List the suspension systems used in EVs.
2. List the suspension systems used in HEVs.
3. Discuss the working of MacPherson suspension system in EVs.
4. Mention the applications of MacPherson suspension system.
5. Discuss the working of double wishbone suspension system in EVs.
6. Mention the characteristics of double wishbone suspension system.
7. Mention the applications of double wishbone suspension system.
8. Mention the applications of semi-trailing arm suspension system.
9. Mention the applications of trailing arm with twist-beam suspension system.
10. Discuss the characteristics of four-link type suspension system.
11. Discuss the characteristics of five-link type suspension system.
12. Mention the applications of multi-link type suspension system.
13. What is electronic air suspension system in EVs?
14. Write a note on regenerative suspension system.

24 BRAKE SYSTEM FOR EVs

UNIT OUTCOMES

Upon successful completion of this module, the student will be able to:

1. Identify the different types of braking system used in EVs and HEVs.
2. Get exposed to ABS.
3. Understand the importance of regenerative braking.

In a vehicle the actuator pedal is released, fuel injection to the engine gets reduced and the vehicle slows down. Then the application of brake further reduces the speed and stops the vehicle.

Electrical energy to the motor reduces when the actuator pedal in an electric vehicle is released. As a result, the speed of the electric car reduces due to friction on the tires, and aerodynamic friction. To completely stop the vehicle additional braking is required. It is known as regenerative braking.

Similar to the IC engine vehicle, the brake system in the electric vehicles shall be disc or drum brake.

Most electric cars use both mechanical and regenerative braking systems together.

Electric vehicle	Brakes used
Mahindra E_2O	Regenerative braking system
Mitsubhishi i MiEV	Front-Disc; Rear-Drum
Renault Zoe	Front-Disc; Rear-Drum
Nissan LEAF	Front-Disc; Rear-Disc
Ford Focus electric	Front-Disc; Rear-Disc
Chevrolet spark EV	Front-Disc; Rear-Disc
BMW i3	Front-Disc (ABS); Rear-Disc (ABS)
Tesla model X & S	Front-Disc (ABS); Rear-Disc (ABS)
Volkswagen e-up	Front-Disc; Rear-Trammels

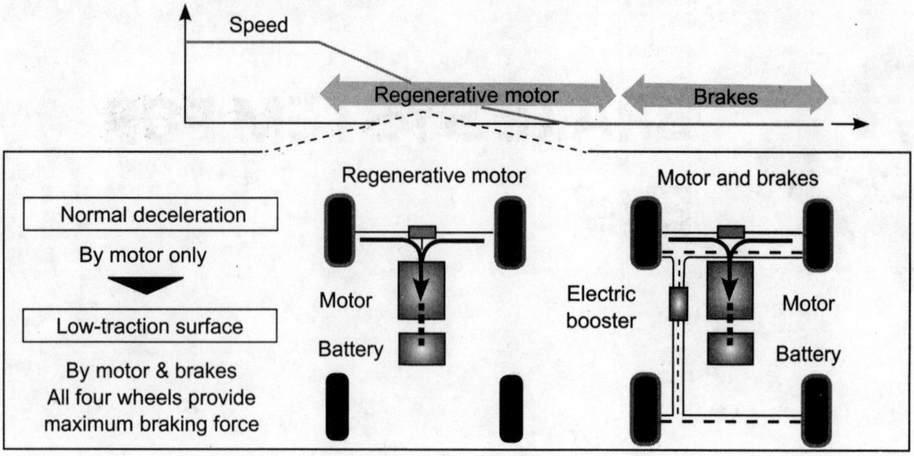

Fig. 24.1: Brake system for EVs

DRUM BRAKE

In a drum brake, braking power is obtained by causing non-rotating shoes to be pushed (by a cam in mechanical brakes or hydraulic pressure in hydraulic brakes or compressed air in air brakes) against the inner surface of a drum that rotates together with the wheel. When the pressure is released, return springs pull the shoes back to their rest position.

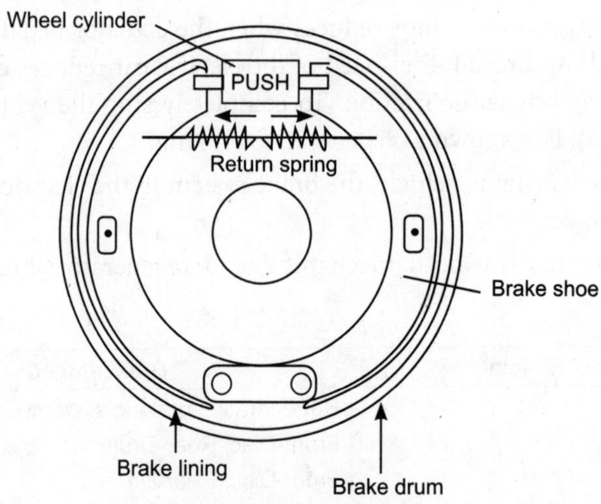

Fig. 24.2: Drum brake

The drum brake consists mainly of the following components:

Components
- Backing plate
- Wheel cylinder
- Brake shoe and lining
- Brae drum

Backing plate

The backing plate is a pressed steel plate bolted to the rear axle housing or rear axle carrier. Since the brake shoes are fitted to the backing plate, all of the braking force acts on the backing plate.

Wheel cylinder

The wheel cylinder is used to expand the brake shoes against the brake drum. One or two wheel cylinders are used for each wheel. Some systems have two pistons (operated by hydraulic pressure) to operate two shoes, one at each side of the wheel cylinder, while other systems have only one piston to operate only one shoe.

Brake shoe and brake lining

The brake shoe is semi-circular in shape. Brake shoes are usually made of steel plates. The brake lining is attached to the shoe by rivets (on large vehicles) or by adhesives (on small vehicles). The material used for lining must have the following qualities:

- good frictional properties
- wear resistance
- heat resistance

Linings were once largely made of asbestos, but the health risks associated with this substance have brought about its replacement with synthetic materials.

Brake drum

The brake drum is generally made of gray cast iron. It is positioned very close to the brake shoe without actually touching it and rotates with the wheel. As the lining is pushed against the inner surface of the drum when the brake is applied, friction heat can reach as high as 200°C to 300°C.

Advantages drum brakes

The drum brake has many advantages as below:

1. Self-applying action
2. Simple hand brake arrangement

3. The drum brake is housed inside the dished area of the road wheel and is thus protected against dirt to a large extent. It is also easy to install a mechanically-operated parking brake.
4. Production and purchase costs are cheaper.

Disadvantages drum brakes

The drum brake has the following disadvantages:

1. Brake fading when hot. Poor heat dissipation may cause brake to fade and also reduce co-efficient of friction between friction lining and brake shoe.
2. Brake inspection requires removal of parts.
3. Self-servo effect.
4. Poor water recovery. Because it has an enclosed design, when the brake cavity gets wet due to rain, floods, or driving over a puddle, the water cannot be expelled right away. The collected water can reduce the frictional properties of the braking system, and this can be dangerous because the vehicle has a decreased stopping ability.

DISC BRAKE

A disc brake basically consists of a cast-iron disc (disc rotor) that rotates with the wheel and fixed friction materials (brake pads) that are pushed against the disc rotor. Braking force is generated by friction between the disc and the disc pads.

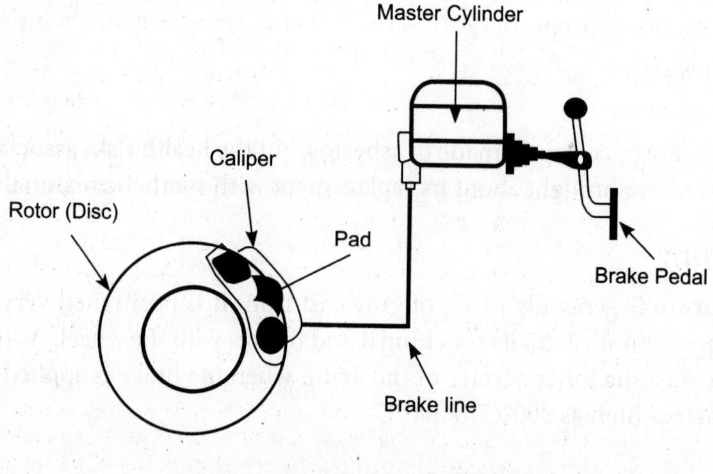

Fig. 24.3: Components of disc brake

COMPONENTS OF DISC BRAKES

A disc brake basically consists of a cast-iron disc (disc rotor), brake pads and caliper.

Disc rotor

Generally, the disc rotor is made of gray cast iron and is either solid or ventilated. The ventilated type disc rotor consists of a pair of hollow discs to ensure good cooling, both to prevent fading and to ensure longer pad life.

Brake pad

A disc pad is usually a baked mixture of metallic fibers and resin containing a small amount of metal powder. This type is called the semi-metallic disc pad. A slit is provided on the rotor side of the pad to indicate the pad thickness (allowable limit) so that the pad wear can be checked easily.

CALIPER

The caliper, also called the cylinder body, holds the pistons and is provided with channels through which the brake fluid is supplied to the cylinders.

Electric cars need hydraulic brakes because hydraulic brakes stop car immediately. In hydraulic systems, the driver doesn't directly activate the master cylinder by pressing on the brake pedal. Instead, the master cylinder is activated by an electric motor or pump that is regulated by a control unit. When the brake pedal is pressed in an electro-hydraulic system, the control unit uses information from a number of sensors to determine how much braking force each wheel needs. The system can then apply the necessary amount of hydraulic pressure to each caliper.

Calipers are grouped into the following types by the way in which they are installed: fixed caliper type and floating caliper type.

Fixed caliper type

The caliper is fixed to the axle or strut. As illustrated in Figure, the fixed caliper is provided with a pair of pistons. Braking force is obtained when the pads are pushed hydraulically by the piston against both ends of the disc rotor.

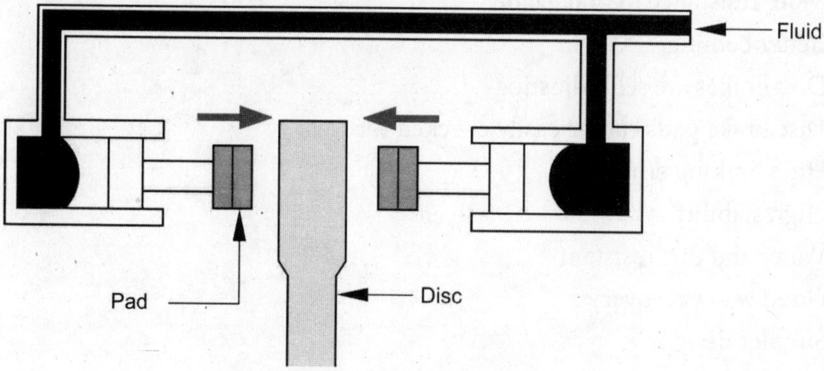

Fig. 24.4: Fixed caliper type

The fixed caliper is the most basic design and ensures accurate operation. However, it requires a large number of components. For this reason, the fixed caliper type disc brakes are used only for some high performance models today.

Floating caliper type

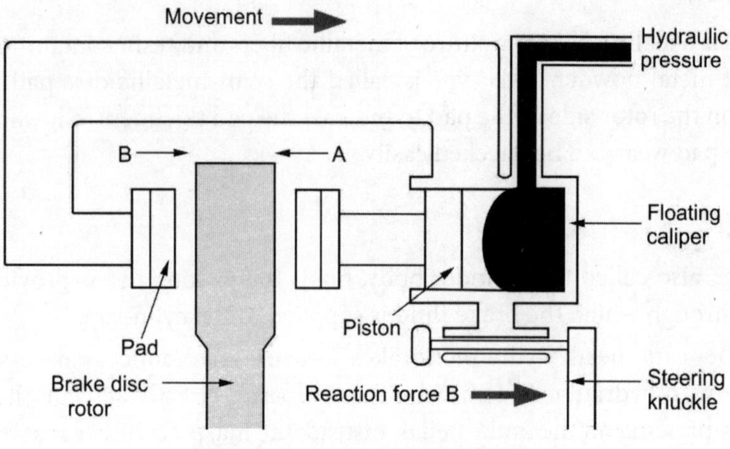

Fig. 24.5: Floating caliper type

As illustrated in Figure, the piston is located in one side of the caliper only. Hydraulic pressure from the master cylinder pushes the piston (force A) and thus presses the pads against the disc rotor. At the same time equal hydraulic pressure (reaction force B) acts on the bottom of the cylinder. This causes the caliper to move to the right and presses the pad located opposite the piston against the disc rotor to exert braking force.

Advantages over drum brakes

The disc brake has many advantages:

1. More resistance to brake fade
2. Better cooling
3. Disc brakes are self-adjusting
4. Disc brake pads can be easily checked for wear
5. High braking efficiency
6. High stability
7. Water and dirt resistant
8. Good water recovery
9. Simpler design

Disadvantages over drum brakes

The disc brake has the following disadvantages over drum brakes:

1. Disc brakes are not as effective at slow speed.
2. The disc brake needs more pressure to work effectively.
3. Size of the disc pad is limited.
4. Pads wear faster than drum brake shoe lining.

ANTI-LOCK BRAKE SYSTEM (ABS)

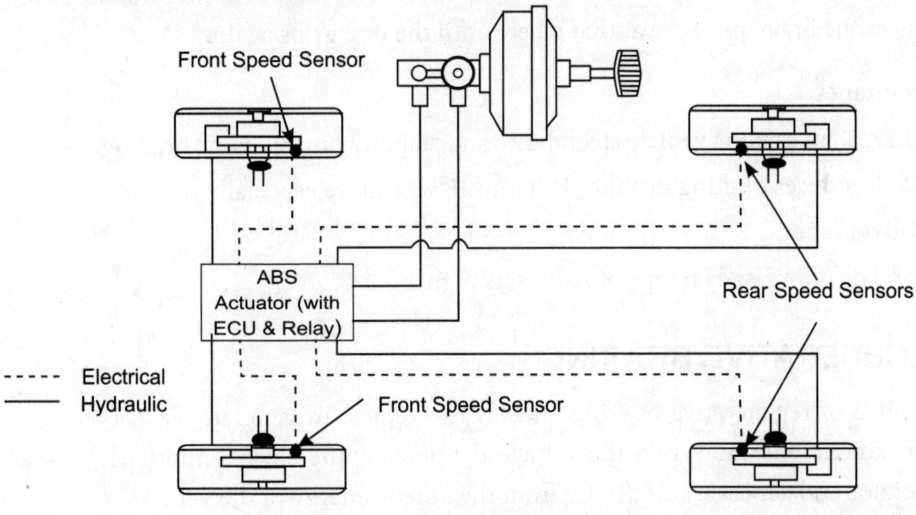

Fig. 24.6: ABS

ABS (Antilock Braking System) is a type of an active safety system of electric vehicles too. It is also known as the anti-skid braking system. This system comes into action when the driver suddenly applies brakes during an emergency or on slippery surfaces.

Need for ABS

Whenever driver suddenly applies brakes to a high-speed vehicle, there is always a danger of wheel lock. Wheel lock means that the respective wheel stops suddenly instead of coming to a halt slowly. Due to wheel lock, the driver loses control over the vehicle and thus fatal accident takes place. In order to avoid such situations, ABS is used. The ABS controls the hydraulic pressure acting on the wheel cylinders to prevent the wheels from locking up. It also maintains directional stability during braking so that the vehicle can be steered.

Components and operation

The heart of the ABS system is an electronic control unit (ECU) which is provided with inputs from sensors and gives outputs to the controls. The sensors are located at each wheel and send pulse generated signals to the ECU. They indicate whether each wheel is revolving and how fast it is turning. The ECU then controls the output of a hydraulic pump assembly. Based on the input signals from the wheel sensors, the ABS system's ECU knows the speed of each wheel. When the brakes are applied, the wheels and the vehicle start to slow down. The ECU monitors the reducing pulses from each of the wheel sensors. If a wheel seems about to lock up, the ECU reduces the brake pressure at that wheel until the tyre grips again.

Advantages

1. ABS maintains vehicle steerability and stability during panic braking.
2. It reduces braking distance by up to 10% or more especially on wet surfaces.

Disadvantages

1. The only disadvantage of ABS is its higher cost.

REGENERATIVE BRAKING

The idea of regenerative braking enables the vehicle to generate electric energy from kinetic energy. When the vehicle decelerates, the electric motor acts as a generator and generates electricity from the kinetic energy of the vehicle.

The energy which is normally lost as frictional heat during braking can be converted into electrical energy. For this purpose the electric motor is operated as a generator. The regenerated energy can be used to recharge the batteries of an EV or HEV. It is important to note that it will not be possible to capture all of the energy available during vehicle braking.

At the same time the generator operation of the electric motor brings about a vehicle braking effect. Once the driver takes his foot off the accelerator pedal, regenerative recovery of energy is activated. Also of significance is the recovery of energy (potential energy) while coasting downhill.

Regenerative braking may yield 10-15% fuel savings.

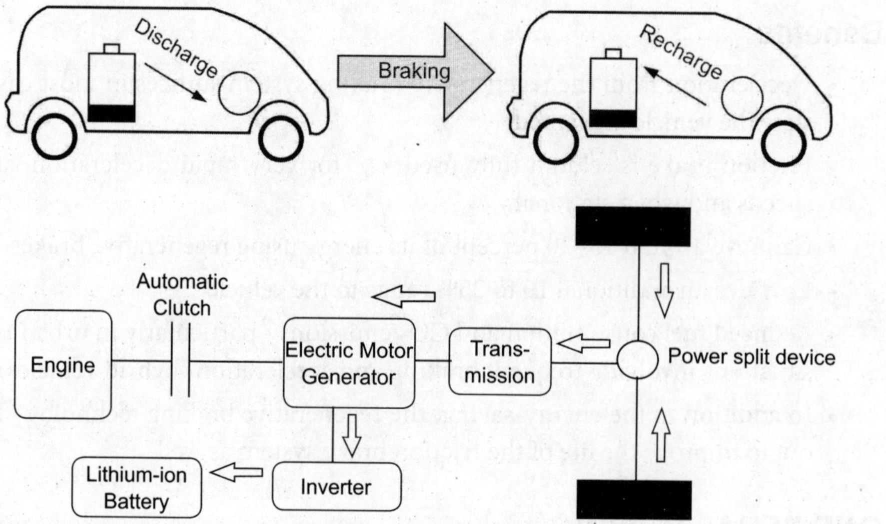

Fig. 24.7: Regenerative braking

As the vehicle stops, friction brakes are also applied to keep the vehicle standstill. There are many factors that affect the effectiveness of regenerative braking. The mass of the vehicle, speed, battery state of charge, etc. are a few of them. Energy recuperation can be used when the vehicle moves down in slop.

Another factor that affects the efficiency of regenerative braking is the drive cycle. For example, on a highway where the speed is almost constant, the chances of energy recuperation are much less.

The regenerative braking technology is getting advanced day by day and it helps out the vehicle to be driven only using one pedal.

Principle

Any permanent magnet motor can operate as either a motor or generator. In all-electrics and hybrids, they are more precisely called a motor/generator (M/G). When an M/G is supplied with electricity it makes mechanical power, when it's supplied with mechanical power, it makes electricity.

When the brake pedal is pressed, the regenerative braking circuit switches the motor so that it now operates in reverse to counter the direction of the wheels. This reversal actually makes it perform like a power generator or dynamo that produces electrical energy. The electricity developed is routed towards the car's storage batteries to recharge them. At higher speeds, regenerative brakes still require the assistance of traditional brake systems to be applied as a backup.

Benefits

- Deceleration from the regenerative braking system suffices in most cases to slow the vehicle as wanted.
- Friction brake is seldom fully used, e.g. for very rapid deceleration, at low speeds and when stationary.
- Can save around 15–20 percent of its energy using regenerative brakes
- Provides an additional 10 to 25% range to the vehicle.
- Reduced fuel consumption and CO_2 emissions - particularly in urban traffic situations involving frequent braking and acceleration (hybrid vehicles).
- In addition to the energy-saving, the regenerative braking technology helps out to improve the life of the friction brake system as well.

ONE PEDAL DRIVING

One-pedal driving allows a driver to bring a vehicle to a full stop without using the brake pedal. In most cases, there is an on-off button that engages this feature. The button activates the one-pedal driving system.

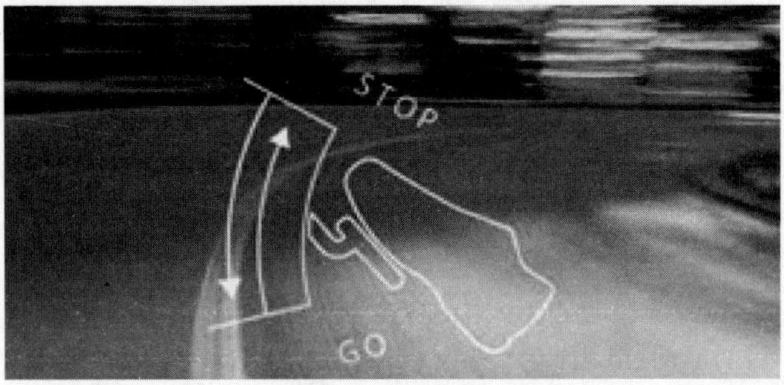

The idea of a single pedal (e-pedal) driving arises with the regenerative braking technology. If both friction braking and regenerative braking is integrated together in the actuator pedal, then the use of brake pedal can be avoided in the vehicle.

One pedal driving method avoids the use of brake pedal in an electric vehicle in normal driving conditions. The single pedal – "e-pedal" – does both the acceleration as well as braking. There is one brake pedal in one pedal driving vehicle to use at emergency. The driver can apply the brakes manually to stop the vehicle in case of an emergency.

Nissan Leaf, Tesla, Chevrolet bolt, etc, have one pedal driving feature in their vehicles.

Advantages of one pedal driving

- It's convenient to use – One we are familiar with the correct position of the e-Pedal, it would be convenient to use the single pedal driving feature of the electric car.
- Single pedal driving provides a smooth deceleration to the vehicle – The software-controlled deceleration would be smoother than the manual deceleration exerted by the driver.

Working of One-Pedal Driving

As the driver anticipates a stop ahead due to a traffic light or a stop sign, they can ease their foot off the accelerator pedal. The vehicle will begin to decelerate at a force of approximately 0.2g (which our bodies experience as gentle deceleration). This deceleration force is equivalent to 20% of full braking force, gradually slowing the car compared to the typical application of the hydraulic brakes. Once the vehicle stops entirely, the hydraulic brakes engage to keep the vehicle at a full stop until the driver presses the accelerator pedal to move forward again.e-Pedal will hold the vehicle in place on grades as steep as 30 percent, all without the driver ever touching the brake pedal.

For Emergency stopping

If an emergency stop is necessary during one-pedal driving, the driver must use the standard hydraulic brakes. No matter the situation, the driver can always apply the standard brakes to bring the vehicle to a stop, whether that be for a pedestrian, vehicle, or any other danger or obstruction on the roadway. One-pedal driving is a convenience feature that the driver can override at any time.

REVIEW QUESTIONS

1. What is regenerative braking?
2. Discuss the types of braking systems suitable for EVs.
3. State the need of ABS.
4. List out the advantages and disadvantages of ABS.
5. Give the benefits of regenerative braking system.
6. Brief about one pedal driving.

25 BEST ELECTRIC AND HYBRID CARS

UNIT OUTCOMES

Upon successful completion of this module, the student will be able to:

1. Identify the best EVs and HEVs

ELECTRIC VEHICLES

Tata Nexon EV

The Nexon EV is the all-electric version of the Tata Nexon compact SUV. Headline numbers include 129hp power, a 312km ARAI-certified range and an 8 year/160,000km warranty on the 30.2kWh Li-ion battery pack. At present, the Tata Nexon EV is sold in select cities and comes priced at a premium to the standard petrol and diesel Nexons.

Pros

- City-friendly performance
- Well-built car. 5 star safety rating in the crash test.
- There is no lag & the car pulls cleanly.
- The suspension is well tuned. The car is comfortable over rough patches, as well as the handling is equally good. Body roll is well sorted.
- Interiors are good.
- Decently feature loaded.
- 205 mm ground clearance can tackle the bad roads with aplomb.
- Low running cost.

Cons

- Not suited to highway.
- The real world range is around 250 km in 'D' mode but if driven spiritedly in 'S' mode it drastically comes down to below 190 km. Will drop even further if driven aggressively.
- Ergonomics could have been better. e.g. the placement of the 12v socket or the driver side hand-rest and few more.
- Tyre noise and the whine of the electric motor are audible.
- Electronic cutoff to avoid wheel-spin should have been provided.
- Upgrading to a better tyre is recommended. The stock tyres lose grip much earlier than the chassis gives up.
- Long term reliability is unknown for this car.
- Auto up/down on the driver's side power window is missing.
- The high floor-pan in rear hinders the comfort of the passenger seating in the middle.

Hyundai Kona Electric, 2019

The Kona Electric is a new favourite among the more accessible EVs. It offers an impressive 258 miles of range, an attractive interior and a long list of tech and safety features. The Kona is also surprisingly quick and entertaining to drive.

Pros

- Long driving range of 258 miles.
- Quick acceleration and sharp handling.
- Comfortable and quite cabin.
- Plenty of standard tech features.

Cons

- Tight rear legroom.
- Limited availability.

Chevrolet Bolt EV, 2017

The Chevrolet Bolt offers huge 238-mile range, quick acceleration and approachable price.

Pros

- Impressive 238 miles of range or more
- Cabin is spacious
- Power and handling make it enjoyable to drive
- Big ouch screen

Cons

- Interior looks and feels cheaper than most.
- Seat feel small and lack cushion depth.
- Ride comfort loses its polish on rougher roads.
- Touch screen has no built-in navigation maps, relies on a paired smarphone.

Volkswagen e-Golf, 2016

The e-Golf drives well, has lots of room for people and cargo, and now offers 125 miles of range.

Pros

- Looks and drives more like a typical car than other EVs.
- Premium interior materials.
- Plenty of trunk space.
- Comfortable and quite ride.

Cons

- Shorter electric range than other EVs.
- Limited availability.

Nissan LEAF, 2019

The current Leaf's much longer range and snappier acceleration are its most substantial enhancements. In the world of cost-effective EVs, the Leaf's game is strong.

Pros

- Quick, smooth acceleration
- Broad compliment of driver assistance features.
- Offers more range than similarly priced EVs.
- Quite driving experience.

Cons

- Lacks a telescoping steering wheel.
- Limited small-item storage.
- The back seats do not fold flat.

Hyundai Ioniq Electric, 2019

The Hyundai Ioniq Electric is a tremendous value for an electric car, both in terms of cost of entry and efficiency. It also offers all the user-friendly technology. But it falls short of class leaders in terms of performance and driving range.

Pros

- One of the most affordable electric vehicles.
- Generous cargo space in black.

- Packed with active driving aids and technology.
- Uses electricity very efficiently.

Cons

- Acceleration lacks punch.
- Back seat is tight and not very comfortable.
- Limited availability.
- Rear visibility is impeded by low-cut, split rear window.

Tesla Model S

The all-electric Tesla Model S offers exceptional performance, range and utility. It proves that EVs can be both eco-conscious and aspirational.

Pros

- Electric range is impressive.
- Wicked quick acceleration across the board.
- Liftback design affords abundant cargo space.

Cons

- Lacks the luxury polish of some similarly priced sedans.
- Small dealer network means few service centers nationwide.
- Large pricing jumps between mechanically identical trim levels.

BMW i3

While its 114-mile range doesn't make it the champion among electric vehicles, the i3 does offer nimble handling, efficient packaging and a premium interior. It costs more than similar EVs.

Pros

- Quick and nimble due to lightweight chassis.
- Well-crafted, contemporary interior has a distinctive style.
- Available range-extender model.

Cons

- Less range than its primary rivals.
- Reverse-hinged rear doors are suboptimal in parking lots.
- Cargo area is not large and has a high load floor.

Chevrolet Volt Plug-in Hybrids, 2016

Chevrolet Volt is a plug-in hybrid with extraordinary electric range. It's capable of going more than 50 miles on a charge before it switches to using gasoline. A sleek design and the latest tech feature round out the Volt's appeal.

Pros

- More all-electric range than most plug-in hybrids.
- Plenty of advanced technology and safety features.
- Nimble and easy to drive in the city

Cons

- Rear seat and luggage area are not as roomy as that of some other models of the same class.
- Interior material quality is disappointing.
- Tricky parking since the car's nose is hard to see.

MINI Countryman Plug-in Hybrid, 2017

The surprisingly quick Mini Countryman S E plug-in hybrid delivers a shot of excitement to a class that's not exactly known for it. This Mini uses its plug-in hybrid system as more of a performance enhancer than a range-extender; indeed, real-world range (electric plus gasoline) is rather paltry at around 240 miles.

Pros

- Exterior and interior design sets it apart from competitors.
- Materials are of higher quality than in subcompact rivals.
- Manual transmission
- Provides comfort driving experience.

Cons

- Limited EV range and grabby brakes
- Front seats are confining
- Cargo area is small.
- Requires premium fuel.

Hyundai Ioniq Plug-In Hybrid, 2017

The Hyundai Ioniq Plug-In Hybrid is just like the regular Ioniq Hybrid, except it has a larger battery that one can recharge for a useful 29 miles of all-electric driving range. Fully charged and filled, it has the capability to travel over 600 miles.

Pros

- Excellent fuel economy and decent all-electric range.
- Long warranty coverage.
- Plenty of features for the money.

Cons

- Feels a bit slow unless going full throttle.
- Road noise can be annoying.
- Stiff, somewhat uncomfortable ride.
- Transmission's shifting is not always smooth.

Honda clarity, 2017

The Honda Clarity plug-in hybrid broadens this model's appeal, as the Clarity used to be fuel cell-only and limited. The Clarity PHEV an excellent city car, with flexible cargo space and a quiet interior, but its infotainment system is aging and it looks like it came from a dystopian future.

Pros

- Comfortable, well-appointed cabin seats
- Solid driving range in all versions except Clarity electric.
- Pleasant ride quality in electric and plug-in hybrid versions.

Cons

- Limited availability.
- Touchscreen infotainment system can be cumbersome to use.
- Polarizing styling.

Toyota Prius Prime, 2016

A plug-in version of the enduringly popular Prius hybrid, the Prius Prime offers 25 miles of electric-only driving range in addition to gas-electric hybrid functionality. There are some drawbacks, though. Passenger and cargo space are limited by hatchback standards, and the Prime is not all that enjoyable to drive.

Pros

- Outstanding fuel economy, with 25 miles of EV range.
- Comfortable front seats.
- Priced lower than most other plug-ins.

Cons

- Slow acceleration and noisy engine.
- Small cargo area.
- Infotainment system's poor layout and smartphone integration.

REVIEW QUESTIONS

1. Compare the pros and cons of various EVs.
2. Compare the pros and cons of various HEVs.

MULTIPLE CHOICE QUESTIONS

ELECTRIC VEHICLES

1. Select one which is not type of electrical cars
   (a) BEV (battery electrical vehicle)
   (b) PHEV (plug- in Hybrid electrical vehicle)
   (c) Hybrid
   (d) UPHVE (ultra PHVE) [Ans (d)]
2. How many types of electrical cars are there?
   (a) 4 (b) 3
   (c) 2 (d) 1 [Ans. (b)]
3. When the brakes are pressed, the motor becomes
   (a) alternator (b) inverter
   (c) converter (d) nothing will happen [Ans. (a)]
4. Who is the brain of electrical cars?
   (a) Gear system (b) Controller
   (c) Governing system (d) inverter [Ans. (b)]
5. Which one the following is not a type of charging in Electrical car?
   (a) AC charging (b) DC charging
   (c) Tap charging (d) Trickle charging [Ans. (c)]
6. Control system in electrical cars is controls the speed by
   (a) Changing the voltage (b) Changing the inductance
   (c) Changing the frequency (d) Changing the capacitance [Ans. (c)]
7. Controller is use for ______ in Electrical Car
   (a) Change the voltage (b) Change the current
   (c) Change the frequency (d) Change the resistance [Ans. (c)]
8. In electrical car power is converted from
   (a) AC to DC (b) Half wave to full wave
   (c) DC to AC (d) Full wave to half wave [Ans. (c)]
9. The slowest method of charging is known as____
   (a) AC charge (b) DC charge
   (c) Trickle charge (d) Dash charge [Ans. (c)]
10. How many types of available for electrical car charging?
    (a) 2 (b) 3 (c) 4 (d) 5 [Ans. (b)]

11. Electric vehicles can only be used as commuter vehicles because of their limited range.
    (a) True (b) False [Ans. (b)]
12. How many approx. kilo-meters are driven by one battery?
    (a) 1 lakh km (b) 1.6 lakh km
    (c) 3.1 lakh km (d) 9 lakh km [Ans. (b)]
13. Battery life of Electrical cars is generally____ years
    (a) 5 (b) 4 (c) 8 (d) 10 [Ans. (c)]
14. Which one is the most popular drive used in EV?
    (a) Permanent magnet synchronous motor drive
    (b) Brushed motor drive
    (c) Both of above
    (d) None of these [Ans. (a)]
15. The braking system used in EV is____
    (a) Hydraulic brake (b) Regenerative brake
    (c) Combination of both of above brake
    (d) None of these [Ans. (c)]
16. Most preferred motor by electrical car makers is
    (a) BLDC (brush less DC motor)(b) IM (induction Motor)
    (c) Both of above (d) None of the above [Ans. (c)]
17. Which kind of battery is good to use in EV?
    (a) Lithium-ion batteries (b) Nickel-metal hybrid batteries
    (c) Lead-acid battery (d) All of them [Ans. (d)]
18. Select one which is not type of the safety of electrical vehicle?
    (a) Protection against electrical shock
    (b) Battery safety
    (c) Chemical hazard
    (d) None of the above [Ans. (d)]
19. Minimum range of charging time of battery of car is_____
    (a) 1 to 2 hours (b) 2 to 4 hours
    (c) 4 to 20 hours (d) 20 to 30 hours [Ans. (c)]
20. The mile range of electrical cars is normally _______ on full charge
    (a) 60 to 100 miles (b) 20 to 50 miles
    (c) 100 to 150 miles (d) 10 to 40 miles [Ans. (a)]
21. Now a days what is the major problem facing by people in EC (electrical car)?
    (a) Car require more maintenance
    (b) Recharging battery takes time

(c) Car is too expensive
(d) All of these [Ans. (b)]

22. Electrical car require _____ maintenance then gas/diesel car.
(a) More (b) Less
(c) Same (d) Nothing to say [Ans. (b)]

23. Which one is the best advantage to owning electrical car?
(a) Better for drive (b) Better for initial cost
(c) Better for environment (d) None of the above [Ans. (c)]

24. What voltage level is available for battery of electrical car?
(a) 21 V to 51 V (b) 12 V to 15 V
(c) 1000 V to 2000 V (d) 100 V to 400 V [Ans. (d)]

25. Which vehicle has smallest number of components?
(a) Traditional vehicle (b) Hybrid vehicle
(c) Electrical vehicle (d) CNG vehicle [Ans. (c)]

26. Who invented the battery?
(a) Alessandro Volta (b) Alexander Bell
(c) Alessandro Bell (d) Tim Southee [Ans. (a)]

27. When was the first electric car invented?
(a) 1830 (b) 1985
(c) 1832 (d) 1945 [Ans. (c)]

28. What country has the most EVs?
(a) China (b) Norway
(c) Iceland (d) United Arab Emirates [Ans. (b)]

29. According to the Department of Energy, what percentage of EV charging happens at home?
(a) 50% (b) 75%
(c) 80% (d) 90% [Ans. (c)]

30. An EV only needs one of the following maintenance jobs done. Which is it?
(a) Oil change (b) Belt replacement
(c) New spark plugs (d) Brake pad inspections [Ans. (d)]

31. Electric vehicles are less expensive to own and operate than conventional, internal combustion engines.
(a) True (b) False [Ans. (a)]

32. A level 1 charger is like plugging into a standard, 220-volt outlet and does not require special equipment or installation. This type of charging is also known as trickle charging.
(a) True (b) False [Ans. (a)]

33. What is a Time of Use Rate (TOU)?
    (a) A rate offered by some utilities to incentivize customers to use electricity during specific times, generally in low demand times
    (b) A rate offered by some utilities that's based on the length of time an electric vehicle is charging
    (c) A rate offered by some utilities to disincentivize the use of electricity

[Ans. (a)

34. Electric vehicles produce fewer emissions than conventional vehicles.
    (a) True (b) False [Ans. (a)]
35. Electric vehicles can only be used as commuter vehicles because of their limited range.
    (a) True (b) False [Ans. (b)]
36. In what year was the first car powered by an electric motor?
    (a) 1911 (b) 1827 (c) 1962 (d) 1899 [Ans. (b)]
37. True or False: A hydrogen fuel cell vehicle is a type of electric vehicle.
    (a) True (b) False [Ans. (a)]
38. Which of these companies is the only one WITHOUT plans for an all-electric pickup truck?
    (a) Toyota (b) GMC (c) Ford (d) Ram [Ans. (d)]
39. Which EV is featured in Avengers: Endgame?
    (a) Jaguar I-Pace (b) Tesla Model X
    (c) Audi E Tron (d) Porsche Tycan [Ans. (c)]
40. What makes the risk of an electric shock from a high-voltage battery possibly more dangerous than that an AC circuit?
    (a) Higher voltage (b) Lower amperage
    (c) Greater available amperage [Ans. (c)]
41. Who coined the term battery?
    (a) George Franklin (b) Benjamin Fernandes
    (c) Benjamin Franklin (d) George Bush [Ans. (c)]
42. What combustion engines can be used in combination with an electric motor?
    (a) this doesn't matter (b) gasoline engines
    (c) diesel engines (d) common rail diesel engines

[Ans. (a)]

HYBRID VEHICLES

1. A hybrid vehicle
    (a) Has a higher top speed (b) Have to be charged every 100km
    (c) Consumes more fuel (d) Consumes less fuel [Ans. (d)]

2. What was the first commercial hybrid car?
   (a) Lexus RX400h (b) Honda Civic Hybrid
   (c) Toyota Prius [Ans. (c)]
3. When was the first hybrid car on the road?
   (a) 1951 (b) 1920
   (c) 2003 (d0 1899 (e) 1992 [Ans. (d)]
4. What is the operating voltage of the Toyota Prius version 2004?
   (a) 104 volts (b) 500 volts
   (c) 50 volts (d0 399 volts (e) 288 volts [Ans. (b)]
5. What is the definition of a hybrid car?
   (a) A car that runs on electricity
   (b) A car that uses two (or more) distinct power sources to propel the vehicle.
   (c) A car that runs on gas
   (d) A car that generates electricity when it brakes [Ans. (b)]
6. What's the difference between a plug-in hybrid and a battery electric vehicle?
   (a) There is no difference
   (b) A plug-in hybrid only accepts AC power, while a battery electric vehicle accepts AC and DC power
   (c) A plug-in hybrid can be powered by either the battery or the gasoline engine. A pure electric vehicle is powered only by the battery
   [Ans. (c)]
7. When did Toyota launch the first hybrid Prius in Japan?
   (a) 1997 (b) 2003 (c) 2000 (d) 2006 [Ans. (a)
8. In a parallel hybrid:
   (a) One engine drives the front, the other the rear axle
   (b) Is the front axle engine driven by the strongest and the rear axle driven by the weakest engine
   (c) The wheels are powered by both engines
   (d) Is the front axle engine driven by the weakest and the rear axle driven by the strongest engine
   (e) Will the wheels be driven by the most powerful engine, this engine is in turn assisted by the less powerful engine [Ans. (c)]
9. In a series-switched hybrid:
   (a) Goes the power through a succession of motors to the wheels
   (b) The engines simultaneously drive the front and the rear axle
   (c) Is the strongest engine in series with the wheels
   (d) Is the weakest engine in series with the wheels [Ans. (a)]

10. What's the big advantage of the combined hybrid?
    (a) You can manage the consumption better
    (b) You can brake harder
    (c) You can accelerate harder
    (d) You can also use only the electric motor
    (e) You can combine both engines [Ans. (d)]
11. Which of the following is NOT the type of hybrid vehicle?
    (a) Plug-in hybrid (b) Parallel hybrid
    (c) Natural gas for vehicles (d) Series hybrid [Ans. (c)]
12. The hybrid electric vehicle consists of:
    (a) Internal combustion engine + electric motor
    (b) Motor electric 1 + Motor electric 2
    (c) NGV engine + Gasoline engine [Ans. (a)]
13. "In this system, the engine is used to supply electrical power to the motor, which then turns the wheels"
    (a) Select the type of hybrid system according to above description.
    (b) Series hybrid (c) Parallel hybrid
    (d) Plug-in hybrid (e) Series-parallel hybrid [Ans. (a)]
14. "The wheels are driven by both the engine and the motor".
    (a) Select the type of hybrid system according to above description.
    (b) Series hybrid (c) Parallel hybrid
    (d) Plug-in hybrid (e) Series-parallel hybrid [Ans. (b)]
15. Select the features of hybrid electric vehicles
    A. Idle stop
    B. EV drive
    C. Motor assist
    D. Regenerative braking
    (a) A & B (b) A & C
    (c) A, B, C & D (d) A [Ans. (c)]
16. The electric motor in a hybrid car can also act as:
    (a) Cooling fan (b) Fuel pump
    (c) Generator [Ans. (c)]
17. Regenerative braking involves
    (a) Nanofibers that repair the surface of brake pads
    (b) Reducing the amount of friction necessary to slow a car
    (c) Reclaiming heat from the brakes and using it for power [Ans. (c)]

18. A -------------- is a vehicle that can run on just the engine, just the batteries, or a combination of the two.
    (a) Mild hybrid (b) Full hybrid
    (c) Fuel cell (d) Assist hybrid [Ans. (b)]
19. Select the WRONG statement
    (a) Toyota produced the insight hybrid
    (b) Hybrid systems rely on very high voltages
    (c) All of the high-voltage cables are covered in orange sleeves for easy identification
    (d) To test high-voltage systems you need a category 3 (CAT III) digital volt ohmmeter [Ans. (a)]
20. Select the CORRECT statement about Integrated Motor Assist (IMA) hybrid system
    (a) Produced by Honda
    (b) This system is the basis for many series-parallel hybrid vehicles
    (c) This system is capable of instantaneously switching from one power source to another or combining the two. [Ans. (a)]
21. Answer in True/False
    A. In electric heavy series-parallel HEV, battery is not used in normal driving.
    B. Parallel HEV has dual axle transmission mechanism.
    C. In straight drive, speed of both the motors is same, in dual motor system.
    (a) True, B) False, C) True (b) True, B) False, C) False
    (c) False, B) False, C) True (d) False, B) True, C) True [Ans. (a)]
22. Answer in True/False
    A. With differential action, there is little sliding and wear of tyres.
    B. Ultra capacitors are high voltage devices.
    C. Fixed gear systems require high motor rating.
    (a) True, B) True, C) False (b) False, B) False, C) True
    (c) False, B) True, C) False (d) False, B) True, C) True [Ans. (b)]
23. Answer in True/False
    A. High power motors cannot be designed for lower voltages.
    B. In fixed gear system, design of motor is very important.
    C. Efficiency in variable gear system is high.
    (a) True, B) True, C) False (b) False, B) False, C) True
    (c) False, B) True, C) False (d) False, B) True, C) True [Ans. (b)]

24. Answer in True/False
    A. At low engine speeds, fuel consumption is high.
    B. In ICEV, we don't operate in optimal operation line.
    C. Complex HEV has 3 propulsion devices
    (a) True, B) False, C) True (b) True, B) False, C) False
    (c) False, B) False, C) True (d) False, B) True, C) True [Ans. (a)]
25. Answer in True/False
    A. In parallel HEV, two motors are used.
    B. In ICE heavy series parallel HEV, only mechanical drive train is active during normal driving.
    C. In front electric rear hybrid complex HEV, no battery charging takes place during lights loads.
    (a) True, B) True, C) False (b) True, B) False, C) False
    (c) False, B) False, C) True (d) False, B) True, C) True [Ans.(d)]
26. By what name are traditionally powered vehicles, equipped with a start-stop system, sometimes also known?
    (a) Micro hybrid (b) Full hybrid
    (c) Hybrid [Ans. (a)]
27. Which vehicle uses a high-voltage battery?
    (a) Electric (b) Hybrid
    (c) Both a & b (d) None of the above [Ans. (b)]
28. Which of the following vehicles produces zero emissions?
    (a) Traditional (b) Hybrid
    (c) Electric [Ans. (c)]
29. What voltage is likely to be available from the battery of an electric vehicle or hybrid?
    (a) 12V (b) 300V
    (c) 40V (d) 55V [Ans. (b)]
30. Answer in True/False
    A. In series HEV, battery can be charged at rest.
    B. In parallel HEV, both drive trains are active during normal driving.
    C. In front hybrid rear electric complex HEV, whole system is active in acceleration mode.
    (a) True, B) True, C) False (b) False, B) True, C) False
    (c) True, B) False, C) True (d) False, B) True, C) True [Ans. (c)]

REFERENCES

1. Robert Bosch GmbH, Bosch Automotive Electrics and Automotive Electronics, Springer, 5th Edition, 2007.
2. V A W Hillier, Powertrain Electronics, Nelson Thomes Ltd, UK, 2006.
3. Ronald K Jordan, Automotive Electronics Handbook, McGraw-Hill, Inc
4. Tom Denton, Automobile Electrical and Electronics Systems, 3rd Edition, Elsevier Butterworth-Heinemann.
5. Colin R. Ferguson, Internal Combustion Engnes, 2nd Edition, John Wiley & Sons. Inc., 2001.
6. Fuad Un-Noor et al. A Comprehensive Study of Key Electric Vehicle (EV) Components, Technologies, Challenges, Impacts, and Future Direction of Development. Energies 2017, 10, 1217; doi:10.3390/en10081217
7. One-Day National Workshop on 'Recent Advances in Automotive Electronics', SAE Indian, Southern India section, Oct.2002.
8. Arumugam S. Ramadhas, Alternate Fuels for Transportation, CRC Press, 2011.
9. Ali Emadi et al., Vehicular Electric Power Systems, Marcel Dekker, Inc, 2004.
10. C.C. Chan and K.T. Chau, Modern Electric Vehicle Technology, Oxford University Press, 2001.
11. Iqbal Husain, Electric and Hybrid vehicles, CRC Press, 2005.
12. Curtis D.Anderson, Electric and Hybrid Cars, 2nd Edition, McFarland & Company, Inc. Publishers, 2010.
13. Allen E.Fuhs, Hybrid Vehicles, CRC Press, 2009.
14. James Larminie and John Lowry, Electric Vehicle Technology Explained, John Wiley & Sons Ltd, 2003.
15. K.T.Chau, Electric Vehicle Machines and drives, IEEE Press, 2015.
16. M J Nunney, Light and Heavy Vehicle Technology, B/H, 2007.
17. Ron Hodkinson and John Fenton, Lightweight Electric/Hybrid Vehicle Design, B/H, 2001.
18. Mehrdad Ehsani, Modern Electric, Hybrid Electric and Fuel Cell Vehicles, CRC Press, 2005.
19. Tom Denton, Electric and Hybrid Vehicles, IMI, 2016.
20. Sandeep Dhameja, Electric Vehicle Battery Systems, Newnes, 2002.

21. ZEBRA batteries, Encyclopedia of Applied Electronics, Springer, 2014.
22. Joseph Beretta, Automotive Electricity, Wiley, 2005.
23. Seth Leittman & Bob Brant, Build your own Electric Vehicle, 2nd edition, McGraw Hill Companies, 2009.
24. Toyota Training Manual, TEAM 2, Fundamentals of Electricity, 1995.
25. Toyota Training Manual, TEAM 2, Fundamentals of Electronics, 1995.
26. Tom Denton, Automobile, Mechanical and Electrical System, Elsevier Ltd., 2011.
27. Uwe Kiencke and Lars Nielsen, Automotive Control Systems, 2nd edition, Springer, 2005.
28. William Ribbens, Understanding Automotive Electronics, 7th edition, B-H, 2012

AND
Web pages related to EVs and HEVs

INDEX